Television in the Nursing Home
*A Case Study of the Media
Consumption Routines and Strategies
of Nursing Home Residents*

Television in the Nursing Home
A Case Study of the Media Consumption Routines and Strategies of Nursing Home Residents

Wendy J. Hajjar, PhD

LONDON AND NEW YORK

First published 1998 by The Haworth Press, Inc.,

2 Park Square, Milton Park, Abingdon, Oxfordshire OX14 4RN
52 Vanderbilt Avenue, New York, NY 10017

Routledge is an imprint of the Taylor & Francis Group, an informa business

First issued in paperback 2020

Copyright © 1998 Taylor & Francis

All rights reserved. No part of this book may be reprinted or reproduced or utilised in any form or by any electronic, mechanical, or other means, now known or hereafter invented, including photocopying and recording, or in any information storage or retrieval system, without permission in writing from the publishers.

Notice:
Product or corporate names may be trademarks or registered trademarks, and are used only for identification and explanation without intent to infringe.

Cover design by Monica L. Seifert.

Library of Congress Cataloging-in-Publication Data

Hajjar, Wendy J.
   Television in the nursing home : a case study of the media consumption routines and strategies of nursing home residents / Wendy J. Hajjar.
     p. cm.
   Includes bibliographical references and index.
   ISBN 0-7890-0293-0 (alk. paper).
   1. Nursing home care. 2. Television and the aged. 3. Nursing homes—Recreational activities.
I. Title.
RA999.R42H35 1998
362.1´6—dc21
                                                  97-43559
                                                     CIP

ISBN 978-0-7890-0293-8 (hbk)
ISBN 978-0-367-60516-2 (pbk)

CONTENTS

Introduction	1
STAGE ONE: ENTERING THE FIELD	5
Chapter 1. Aging and Media Use	7
Chapter 2. Television and Social Life in the Nursing Home	13
Chapter 3. Ethnographic Methodology	21
Chapter 4. A Day in the Nursing Home	31
Summary of Stage One	43
STAGE TWO: NARROWING THE FOCUS	47
Chapter 5. Program Preferences and Routines	49
Chapter 6. Roommates and Coordination	57
Chapter 7. Key Informants	65
Summary of Stage Two	85
STAGE THREE: ANALYSIS AND CONCLUSIONS	87
Chapter 8. The Viewing Stance	89
Chapter 9. Control and Selectivity	101
Chapter 10. Minimizing the Negatives	117
Chapter 11. Storytelling: Accentuating the Positive	125
Chapter 12. Conclusions and Recommendations	135
Bibliography	143
Index	149

ABOUT THE AUTHOR

Wendy J. Hajjar, PhD, is Associate Professor of Communications at the University of New Orleans and is involved with such interdisciplinary programs as the new Gerontology Certificate Program and the Women and Gender Studies Program. A member of several professional societies, Dr. Hajjar has chaired panels and presented papers at professional meetings of the International Communication Association, the National Communication Association, and the Gerontological Society of America. Since 1991, she has designed and developed several graduate and undergraduate courses at the University of New Orleans. She is editor of *Prescription for Life* and has written book chapters in *Cross-Cultural Communication and Aging in the United States* and *Book of Days*. Dr. Hajjar is a 1993 graduate of Purdue University.

Introduction

Our society currently is facing the problem of how to care for its rapidly expanding elderly population. Advances in medical technology and improvements in diet and general standard of living have resulted in the unprecedented emergence of a fourth generation—a generation of very old who, with high probability, will live to experience great-grandparenthood (the fourth generation). This change in family structure distinguishes today's elders from their parents, or any previous cohort. Many are living long enough to see their children reach retirement age. Caregivers, who often are female family members not paid for their services, tend to come from a population segment with the fewest resources to expend. By the time older parents need assisted living, many caregivers are unable to provide services at home.

The emergence of a fourth generation is stimulating rapid development in the field of gerontology, a comparatively young area of medical science. Gerontology's practical training grounds are the institutions that provide support services for the aged who need daily assistance, and include day care and long-term nursing care facilities. As the percentage of elderly in the general population increases, the number of facilities devoted to care of the frail elderly continues a pattern of steady growth maintained throughout this century. This pattern of growth has prompted discussion as to what long-term care services will be required in the future.

While medical care has taken precedence in the design and operation of nursing facilities, the social needs of long-term care residents have received much less attention. Television has slipped into this void, and television use has become the single most prevalent activity, a situation that is met with a kind of reluctant acceptance by most caregivers. While some have asked why television use is so high, or even what deleterious consequences might result from so much exposure to the medium, it might be more profitable to ask, "Why not?" With its ease of delivery and constant availability, television provides stimulation, information, and entertainment that demands comparatively little from its older consumers for all the services it delivers. While long-term care facilities need to continue to develop means for institutional residents to engage in productive social activity, the deeper question that frames this study is: To what degree does television use qualify as productive social activity in long-term care?

When evaluated against other academic disciplines, it is clear that both gerontology and communication are still relatively new disciplines, with most of the significant work accomplished in only the last thirty years. In that time, concepts and measurement techniques have rapidly become more sophisticated, yet theoretical development betrays the youth of both disciplines. In the gerontological literature, high television use is widely assumed to be problematic, while in the mass communication literature it is clear the very old have been largely ignored both by the media industries and by researchers alike. This study focuses on the area of media consumption in the nursing home to better understand why television use is so high, whether high television use is problematic to its users, and how it fits into everyday life in a long-term care facility.

The nursing home context facilitates the examination of media use in an institution, but it also facilitates research into the communication practices of the very old. Paradoxically, the elderly constitute the demographic group with the longest history with the mass media, resulting in some of the deepest loyalties for print and electronic media channels, genres, programs, and personalities. But they are served with the least regard by the media industries, due largely to their lack of economic leverage. However, the daily activities of nursing home residents are under constant surveillance, and interventions are routinely used to promote health and well being. This context holds the potential for identifying the particular needs of people in long-term care, for the development of new media designed specifically for use by the very old, and for the design of media-centered activities that recognize the potential for therapeutic use of communication technologies in the nursing home. To that end, this report offers practical suggestions for assessment of communication practices and activity intervention.

Furthermore, theoretical development for both gerontology and communication studies emerges from sustained examination of situated members of an interacting social group. The ability to examine members' accounts of their everyday activities, to observe their communication behavior, and to ask questions about the social life in a nursing home allows the opportunity to address simultaneously some assumptions and theories about aging, institutionalization, and media use. This report establishes that television consumption, once thought to be problematic, should be seen as desirable and necessary. It is a resource that, along with entertainment and information, also provides opportunities for comfort, self-expression, and sociality.

With these matters in mind, this document comprises twelve chapters, organized into three units that represent a three-stage ethnographic research process with an increasingly narrowed focus on selected elements of everyday communication practices. Stage One consists of four chapters that establish the background and the process of gaining entry to the nursing home as a unique research site. Chapters 1 and 2 review previous research conducted in the areas of media and aging, and social life in the nursing home. Chapter 3 discusses an appropriate methodology to support research questions about aging, media use, and institutional life. The first stage ends with Chapter 4, titled "A Day in the Nursing Home," introducing a group of key residents and their typical media routines.

Stage Two of the research process involves moving from general observations to sustained focus on the factors that influence preferences for certain media programs and media-related routines. This stage identifies factors that ultimately determine both the quantity and the pleasure of the media consumption experience. Chapter 5 reports results from a survey of media preferences and everyday social routines. Chapter 6 focuses on the different roommate styles that are observed, raising questions about the nature of coordinated activity in the institution. Stage Two concludes with Chapter 7, a closer look at the key resident informants of this study and the logical premises that guide their everyday communication activities.

Stage Three focuses on the conceptual field of media consumption routines, examining the strategic media activities where individual resources are mobilized toward the aim of countering the negative aspects of institutional life. Chapter 8 distinguishes different styles of consumption and the roommate relationships they engender. Chapter 9 discusses the connection between resources, selectivity, and individual control, suggesting the limitations and responses made by long-term residents. Chapter 10 probes the strategic aspects of media routines used to counter the perceived negatives of institutional life, and Chapter 11 on the positive uses of media to enhance status and improve quality of life in a care facility. Stage Three concludes with Chapter 12, a summary of the results, discussion of theoretical implications, and recommendations for care providers and future facility design.

STAGE ONE: ENTERING THE FIELD

This project is designed with two goals in mind: to investigate the phenomenon of high television use among the old, and to examine the practices of media use within the nursing home as a distinct institutional social world. To further that end, this section establishes what is known about television and aging and why high television use among the aged has been portrayed as problematic. Addressing what is known about the particular communicative context of the nursing home, television use is situated within the communication needs of the aged in an institution where new communicative relations are considered essential to successful transition into long-term care. The unique requirements of residents of long-term care are addressed in order to outline the procedures used to compile an ethnography of the communication practices of a particular nursing home. Stage One ends with a narrative of a composite day that introduces typical media routines of a group of key informants—nursing home residents who have successfully adapted to long-term care.

Chapter 1

Aging and Media Use

Although the problem of media use in the nursing home has not previously been directly addressed, research on media and aging began to appear in the 1960s, shortly after television had come into wide usage in the United States. By the late 1970s, reviews began to suggest the importance of television and aging (Atkin, 1976; Kubey, 1980), as television came to supplant the use of other media. From the time it was introduced, television, more than any other medium, has had a special appeal for the aged. Even studies conducted some thirty years ago report the elderly using television more than any demographic group (Beyer and Woods, 1963; Cowgill and Baulch, 1962; Schramm, 1969), and more recent findings confirm that a trend of high consumption persists (Altergott, 1988; Mundorf and Brownell, 1990), with television ranking as the most prevalent and the most time-consuming activity in older adults.

High consumption of television is not limited to the aged population in the United States either. Altergott's 1988 volume of time budget studies introduces data from nine cultures in eight industrialized countries, which indicate that television is also the most prevalent activity among the aged wherever it is readily available. How older people budget their time in daily activities reflects a wide variety of needs and problems as well as tastes and interests. But common to most of the elderly studied is an increase in the time spent in tasks associated with daily living, self-care, and the amount of time spent in the home. Consistent with increased time spent in the home is an almost universal increase in time spent with mass media, predominantly television (Peterson, 1982).

Reports that the aged spend large amounts of time with television have prompted research into the medium's negative effects, with reports that high consumption of television is related to problems such as lowered self-concept (Korzenny and Nuendorf, 1980), increased fear of crime (Gerbner and Gross, 1976), and the belief that old people are a "vanishing breed" (Gerbner et al., 1980). Francher (1973) even argues that depression resulting from so much time exposed to youth-oriented media can produce anxieties that cause the aged to exhibit early signs of dementia. The high use of media, television in particular, is said to make the elderly especially vulnerable to its effects, shaping self-concept and worldview in the absence of contradictory truths.

However, surveys of older television viewers do not reveal the same negativity evident in other research. Survey respondents indicate they take the mass media seriously and they feel positively toward the television environment in general (Bliese, 1982). According to some studies, genre preferences in the over-sixty-five group are said to lean toward realism (Kubey, 1980), and elderly audiences tend to focus on the educational benefits when they evaluate media content. They prefer news and public affairs programming, watching television for world news, and reading newspapers for local information (Kubey, 1980; Real, Anderson, and Harrington, 1980; Schreiber and Boyd, 1980). Older television viewers also watch quiz shows to sharpen their intellectual abilities, and how-to programs to learn new skills (Bliese, 1982). They are somewhat conservative in their program choices, preferring realistic drama to situation comedy (Atkin, 1976; Bliese, 1982). Just as television use and newspaper consumption show an increase among this age group, movie attendance and consumption of radio and popular music decline (Atkin, 1976). Meyersohn (1961) is often quoted for his three conditions predisposing the elderly to televison viewing: sedentariness, more leisure time, and fewer ties with the social world.

Contrasting sharply with the positive view of media conveyed in surveys of older consumers, however, theories of media use among the elderly tend to portray high television consumption as problematic. By placing television within the context of other communicative activities, the function of each activity is evaluated under the assumption that low levels of interpersonal interaction explain high television use in this group.

The approach used to evaluate communicative activities considers that the activities an individual chooses will be limited by structural constraints, deficits that limit the ability and the opportunity to communicate with others. When constraints such as retirement, death of a loved one, or relocation to a nursing home occur, substitute activities will need to be found to fill the gap left by the inevitable loss of interactants (Graney, 1975; Oyer and Oyer, 1976). In addition, physical decrement and sensory impairment such as the loss of hearing, sight, and mobility also affect the ability to communicate with others. These are also considered structural constraints, or deficits, that predispose high television use as a substitute for other activities. Television, with its redundancy of aural and visual information, fills in perceptual gaps left by sensory loss, replacing single-channel media that provide audio or visual information, but not both (Kubey, 1980).

The functionalist approach used most often to study communication and aging is known as activity theory, which states that morale is directly related to the level of social interaction (Havighurst and Albrecht, 1953). Social interaction provides necessary role support to maintain a positive self-image (Creecey and Wright, 1979), a theoretical premise that has been widely tested and affirmed in research on the aged. But the relationship posed between television use, other media, and social interaction among the aged still remains open to question. Social disengagement and activity substitution explanations are said to account for the well-documented increase in television viewing and the reduction of other social activities with age, but there are problems with both of these explanations.

Implying that the elderly choose to dissociate from the social environment as a healthy adjustment to aging and in recognition of impending death, high television use has also been labelled social disengagement or withdrawal. Because each activity substitution is seen as less effective in meeting the void left by a lost activity, and because aging is accompanied by a more generalized loss of energy, the concept of disengagement is used to explain why the overall number of social activities declines with age and results in television as a substitute. It has even been suggested that the inevitable decline in the amount of interaction will have less impact on the self-concept of the individual who is well-adjusted and prepared to face the losses associated with aging and impending death (Erikson, 1969; Peck, 1969). This explanation is not well-supported in the literature, however, and Bliese (1982) and Altergott (1988) both argue that the aged do not desire disengagement, but are forced to disengage through social isolation.

Graney and Graney (1974) were among the first to challenge the basic notion of decline inherent in the concept of disengagement. Based on panel studies they conducted, they argue for a substitution model, noting that older adults who experience decrement in one communication activity tend to seek and find functional alternatives where losses do not count against them as severely. Research suggests that the primary alternative tends to be television viewing which, as Schramm initially suggested, serves to combat progressive disengagement by keeping older people in touch with the environment. According to Altergott (1988), the resulting effect of disengagement on society is the "privatization" of the aged, who are relegated to diminished social roles and only allowed to function narrowly within a domestic sphere of activity.

With the activity substitution explanation, social activity losses lead to a lowered self-concept if appropriate alternatives are not found. In this framework, television is conceptualized as an activity substitute that may be judged less satisfying than the social activities lost. Atchley argues, however, that the theory suffers from an assumption of homeostasis. The theory assumes that when changes associated with aging occur, the typical response of the aging individual is to restore equilibrium by substituting another activity. He notes, however, that aging appears highly pathological within a theory that is supposed to objectively account for its effects (Atchley, 1989).

According to proponents of these views, television viewing has a limited place in a mentally healthy lifestyle. Although the aged may have more leisure time than younger people, and may watch more television than any other demographic age group, this is typically cast as a symptom of an unhealthy style of interaction. Throughout the research, a relationship is posited between social interaction and media consumption. However, of fundamental importance here is that research has not established that the elderly person who is socially inactive is also likely to be the heaviest television consumer.

Furthermore, the theory reduces all television use to a single function of social utility, which is presented as a dysfunctional alternative to healthy communication. Describing television use largely as a time filler, theorists then disagree about whether television viewing ultimately constitutes evidence of social withdrawal or a feeble attempt to remain socially integrated (Bettinghaus and Bettinghaus, 1976; Meyersohn, 1961; Schramm, 1969).

An assumption of the inevitability of physical decrement pervades the literature on aging and television use, supported by aggregate survey data that invite unwarranted conclusions about social disengagement as a normative condition of aging. The measurable decline in communication activity is explained as progressive social detachment, despite the fact that individuals typically experience only modest declines in communication activity until immediately prior to death, a period when communication activity does decline more rapidly (Graney and Graney, 1974). But despite problems with developmental theories of aging, no other explanation has been proposed to account for the high levels of media use among the aged.

However, with results from nearly twenty years of study, currently there are data available on the media use of two distinct cohorts, data that undermine the premises of social disengagement. In 1980, Schreiber and Boyd reported that the young elderly (sixty to seventy years) rely more heavily on television than the older members of their sample, and between ages seventy and seventy-six, "a change in media [use] patterns is evident" (p. 67). Although they are careful to point out that this may be due to older respondents' lack of experience with the medium, such reports have been taken as evidence that television consumption drops off in the mid-seventies age group (Atkin, 1976; Schramm, 1969). More recent work refutes this assumption, showing that observed decreases are minor and accounted for in slight increases in time spent in personal care routines, not the result of a desire for withdrawal or disengagement from the social world (Altergott, 1988).

Even with a strong predisposition to television, aging alone does not adequately explain television use when considered against other potential time fillers. Research attempting to address motivations for media choices considers self-reports of media use and the gratifications obtained in terms of the multiple functions that media serve in the lives of the elderly. The most comprehensive study of media gratification of the aged to date (Bliese, 1982) contradicts the assumption that high television use fills only one function for the aged. She argues that media serve the same functions for the aged as for other members of the general population, but that particular functions will take on more or less importance as a person ages.

Bliese's findings include activity substitution as one of ten observed functions. The others include learning and intellectual stimulation, company and safety, entertainment, and gathering information for later conversations. The question of whether social withdrawal occurs is addressed in the temporal dimensions implied in some of the ten functions. The functions related to learning or information gathering for later use imply the expectation of a future focused beyond the immediate communicative event, and belie a disengagement explanation.

However, the social reality of aging is that people do tend to become more sedentary, more dependent, and more isolated with age. But rather than focusing on the deficits of aging, such as the loss of functions and interactants, the losses can more profitably be seen as companion processes to aging, not a normative model. Normal aging may include loss of relations, loss of function, and loss of opportunity. But instead of assuming deficits that are not universal, it is more useful to inventory the resources that remain. Resources, in this case, include the tangible assets such as money and property, but they also include the less tangible assets such as knowledge, relationships, employment or job skills, hobbies, mobility, hearing, and vision. From a resource perspective, older adults that lose some of these resources and yet still manage to find substitute activities to fulfill their needs can be said to strategically maximize the resources that are available toward maintaining a level of consistency in daily activities. If the absolute number of activities declines with age, then, it does not necessarily result in a loss of self-esteem or other negative consequences.

Chapter 2

Television and Social Life in the Nursing Home

Not all elderly will end up in long-term care, but as one ages the likelihood increases. Although at any given time only about 5 percent of the population over sixty-five are in nursing homes (Atchley, 1977; Howsden, 1981; Kayser-Jones, 1981; Vladeck, 1980), this figure is deceptively low, as it obscures the turnover rate of the large numbers of people who die soon after entry (Ingram and Barry, 1977; Kane and Kane, 1982; Kastenbaum and Candy, 1973; Wingard, Jones, and Kaplan, 1987) and quickly exit long-term care. Thus the nursing home functions as a long-term care facility for some, but for others it serves as hospice or recuperative center. At least 20 percent of the population over eighty-five are currently in long-term care, and as age increases, so does the likelihood of residing in a nursing home. The likelihood of dying in a nursing home is especially high (Shield, 1988).

Because the need for nursing homes is fairly new, with most of their growth since 1969 (Vladeck, 1980), and because the fastest growing segment of the population is the oldest group—the frail elderly over eighty-five (Shield, 1988)—it is difficult to predict accurately the number of people who will need long-term care in the near future. Factoring out those who will manage assisted living in private homes, estimates for nursing facility needs are consistently high, and project the expansion to at least twice as many beds between the 1990s and the year 2010, when a majority of the population will be fifty or older. Predicting rapid growth long into the next millenium, Kemper and Murtaugh (1991) estimate that of the 2.2 million Americans who turned sixty-five in 1990, 43 percent are expected to enter a nursing home at some time, and 9 percent or more will live there for at least five years—probably the last five years of their lives.

The typical long-term nursing home resident currently stays an average of 2.6 years, has three or more chronic conditions, is female, eighty years old, white, and widowed (Vladeck, 1980). Fewer than half of nursing home residents are ambulatory. About one-third are partially incontinent, about one-third need assistance eating, and two-thirds need assistance bathing and dressing (Shield, 1988). Reviewing the literature on long-term care utilization, Wingard, Jones, and Kaplan (1987) discuss the variables that identify the population most likely to require institutionalization, concluding that age, sex, availability of caregivers, and functional status are the most significant contributors. Thus the typical resident is a woman who has outlived her spouse and has several medical problems that prevent her from being able to manage her own care. Before entering a facility, she has probably exhausted her financial and familial support resources, and she has entered the institution because she has no other option. At the time she enters the institution, she is probably watching more than six hours of television most days, usually by herself.

It is useful to remain skeptical of generalizations based on simplistic models of aging, and to reevaluate effects that might be attributable to a cohort difference, an artifact of survey data, or some other extraneous source. Despite these concerns, all new residents of a nursing home can expect communicative relations to undergo significant upheaval upon entry. Whether permanent or temporary, the change of residence means almost complete loss of personal posessions and a radical restructuring of daily routines. It means new caretakers will assume control over multiple activities of daily living, resulting in a loss of privacy and a forced intimacy with caregivers and other residents. To thrive, residents will have to adapt fairly quickly to the new environment, getting their needs met with compromise and negotiation while attempting to maintain some sense of control. In the face of such upheaval, media habits are one of the few activity options that can remain fairly consistent.

Sigman (1982) discusses the importance of peer group interaction for the transitional phase of nursing home institutionalization. Appropriate social behaviors, including the ability to learn and adhere to new rules and to develop new social outlets are considered important accomplishments for the newly admitted. Because orientation protocols determine placement according to level of care and the unit of the facility that will offer the best fit, future treatment and services are also reliant on this all-important transition. Caregivers typically promote socialization to aid in the adjustment process. But the development of new friendships is a goal too ambitious for most new nursing home admittees. Tesch, Whitbourne, and Nehrke (1981) also find that nursing home residents derive less satisfaction from new friends made in the nursing home than from interaction with friends on the outside, but friendships initiated in the nursing home are an important predictor of overall satisfaction with the environment.

Chown (1981) argues, however, that enforced sociability in the adjustment to institutional life is less beneficial to residents than the provision of opportunities to be social. She suggests that residents also need the freedom to choose whether to be social or not in order to maintain a sense of individual control. Of course, opportunities to develop mutually satisfying reciprocal relationships provide the most promise for new friendships to develop. And reciprocal relations are most likely to occur between nursing home roommates because of the opportunities afforded for interaction. But Bitzan and Kruzick (1990) find that when nursing home roommates do not develop close ties, they tend to look elsewhere in the facility for friendships. The perception of reciprocity in a relationship is most critical in deriving any benefits of friendship (Arling, 1976; Mitchell and Acuff, 1982; Nussbaum, 1983).

Relationships with staff members, physicians, and caregivers, as well as family members, and perhaps any others who exhibit greater competency will be perceived as less than reciprocal, however. Although Moss and Pfohl (1988) find that staff visits with residents when they are off duty significantly improve morale of residents, they attribute the improvement to the elevation of status of the resident from the role of patient to friend, offsetting the lowered self-esteem that results from exclusively nonreciprocal institutional interaction.

The ability to seek out new friendships in the institution, however, is entirely resource dependent. Mobility, for example, is one resource that allows relationship development outside of the roommate and caregiver ties, making friendship development most difficult for those who are least ambulatory. Status differences prior to institutionalization and the nature of the resident's prior social life and repertoire of social skills can also be expected to influence socialization patterns. Women are more likely than men to seek out new friends in the nursing home (Bitzan and Kruzick, 1990). But whether women have greater social needs, more highly developed social skills, or some other social asset is not known.

As the last chapter indicates, television is most often conceptualized as a second-rate substitute for the intimacy of friendship in the literature on communication and aging. But these conclusions are drawn from assessment of the relative frequency of interpersonal interaction versus time spent with media. However, the quantity of time matters much less to nursing home residents than the quality of each interaction. Furthermore, a measure of the frequency of social contact confounds close friends and confidants with relatives, acquaintances, and caregivers. Chown (1981) argues that the research on friendship and aging has been too focused on the general social conditions of aging rather than on specific, satisfying relationships among elders. She contends that the quality of the relationship will have greater impact on morale than the frequency of interaction.

But the fundamental issue that resurfaces in the communication and aging literature is the conceptualization of media consumption as a functional alternative to sociality. This perspective does not consider the quality of interactions, only the relative frequencies of each communicative activity. Instances where the act of media consumption is in itself a social phenomenon can dispel the notion that all acts of media use are on some level equivalent, and equally impoverished. Furthermore, development of a framework to examine the social aspects of media use in a nursing home requires recognition of the unique demands of an institutional environment. If, as Bliese and others argue, media use does not substitute for interaction, a model that better captures the relationship of media, aging, and sociality in long-term care is warranted.

James Lull's (1980) descriptive typology of social uses of media in the home derived from ethnographic study of family television is such a model. In addition to the four gratification components found in individual media use—diversion, personal relationships, personal identity, and surveillance (McQuail, Blumer, and Brown, 1972)—Lull finds six additional social uses of television. Two of the components of the model he describes as structural, and four as relational. This framework is a useful starting point for describing media use in the nursing home. But examination of the nursing home interaction should yield another level of analysis as well, registering an institutional dynamic in addition to the individual and domestic social uses of media.

Structural uses of media, according to Lull, include both environmental and regulative dimensions. As environmental resources, audio and visual media tend to move in and out of prominence, with household members choosing at any given time where to focus their attention. Regulative uses include punctuation of units of time and activity scheduling. Mealtime, bedtime, time for work, and even activities that take place outside the home demonstrate a regulative dimension that is punctuated by media scheduling. In addition, conversation is routinely regulated by television viewing, including the familiar domestic pattern of delaying conversation until commercial breaks. Because television can be used as a reward granted by authority, or a privilege that can be withdrawn, the structural components are expected to exert greater force in an institutional setting where rules and policies impose a distinct regulative domain.

Relational uses, according to Lull, include four areas: communication facilitation, affiliation/avoidance, social learning, and competence/dominance. Communication facilitation occurs through the communicative use of the common ground of shared media experience. Affiliation/avoidance occurs through shared proximity, and by decreasing the demand for conversation with others. Social learning occurs through the resource potential of media content. The demonstration of competence/dominance occurs through regulating the consumption of others, anticipating program outcomes, comparing oneself with role portrayals, and being more informed on an issue than other household members.

Lull's four relational uses can reveal important dimensions of sociality in the institution. Because previous research establishes that the opportunity variables (homophily and proximity) tend to set the stage for relationships to develop between aged adults (Chown,

1981), similarities in media preferences may demonstrate taste homophily, or perceived similarities based on shared media preferences. And shared consumption routines can demonstrate whether proximity in media use allows nursing home residents to maximally develop social contacts necessary to the maintenance of a positive self-concept without the added pressure that new friendships are expected.

Sharing media preferences, consumption patterns, and practices is a group phenomenon known as a taste culture (McQuail, 1987) or what Radway (1984) refers to as an interpretive community. In addition to sharing content or genre preferences, members of a taste culture are likely to share other perspectives, including explanatory schemes or interpretive frames. Thus it is within a taste culture or interpretive community that meaningful interaction is likely to develop.

According to Lull (1980), the social uses typology is constructed on the belief that social actors actively employ the tools of communication to purposefully construct their social realities. It should also be noted that the functional model on which much of the communication and aging research is based also assumes that an individual freely determines the constitution of his/her own communicative environment. While this may be more true in the case of the aged in private residence, it is an assumption that should be questioned in the institutional setting, where activities are often determined not by individual choice but by institutional demand. Yet, whether or not institutional residents selectively use mass communication or exert any control over the media environment, and whether the issue of control alters the experience, are central issues to be explored before accepting a conceptualization of the individual as a free agent and the mass media as a set of resources in one's control. What it means to communicate with others and what it means to use television will naturally reflect these shifts in control.

Thus, a major concern in looking at sociality and media consumption in the institution is the notion of individual choice versus administrative control. Particularly salient for individuals institutionalized against their will is the degree to which any resident is able to exercise free choice in determining any of the activities that comprise the social schedule. If social interaction is considered to be a complex system comprising media consumption as well as other forms of interaction, the research must focus on the criteria and constraints that one faces in making (or the denial of) such choices.

Older adults face a variety of constraints in their choices of activities, whether living independently or in an institutional setting. Resources such as economics and mobility that impact other social activities also impinge on the degree of freedom exercised in media opportunities as well. In the institution these limitations are compounded by rules and policies imposed by an administration whose needs and goals differ significantly from those of its residents.

Sigman's (1982) research introduces provocative questions regarding the degree of choice nursing home residents exercise in the decision to participate in social activities. He argues that participation is more related to maintaining an appearance of competency than a desire for the benefits derived from social interaction. Stated another way, the primary benefit derived from social interaction may be the appearance of competency through association with competent others.

Thus, the motivation that one has for participating in any social activity has to be considered before assuming its potential benefits. The desire for some measure of control, even in the most mundane areas of social life, may override any perceived benefits of social contact. And whether participation is actively sought or passively engaged is perhaps a more significant indicator of competency. One who actively chooses isolation or withdrawal may feel better about this choice, and hence derive greater benefit from the experience, than one who is participating in activities out of a sense of obligation. Inferences drawn about all social participation require qualification of the meaning of the act from the participant's own point of view.

Atchley's (1988) continuity theory of aging, used here to aid in the identification of the resources of nursing home residents, considers the processes of aging to be normal, including constraints on social interaction in later life. Whereas the losses associated with institutionalization may require adaptation and change, a basic structure underlying behavior persists. According to Atchley, the basic continuity structure is coherent, with a logical relation of parts. In making adaptive choices, older adults attempt to preserve existing continuity structures by applying familiar strategies in adapting to unfamiliar settings.

Examining communication patterns within established relationships provides clues about the importance of opportunities to be social. In this context, a perspective for examining television use in the nursing home includes the examination of relationships and social events which, at a minimum, can be seen to provide opportunities for conversation to develop, and at a maximum, can allow the positive benefits of role support, continuity, and self-fulfillment.

Chapter 3

Ethnographic Methodology

The nursing home population requires methods sensitive to the unique abilities and limitations of this subject group. Because researchers need to anticipate deficits in hearing, vision, writing, energy, and memory, as well as the inevitable intrusion of pain and discomfort, many traditional research strategies are not viable in this setting. Yet care must still be taken to be as objective as possible and to avoid compromising results. To overcome communication barriers, Keith (1986) advocates the use of anthropological methods that allow for maximum discovery over time, adopting nonintrusive techniques sensitive to an older individual's needs. To engage with subjects on their own terms, a flexible research plan that includes an extended period of fieldwork is guided by a protocol that specifies objectives, but does not overly predetermine procedures. Following standard participant observation fieldwork the primary data are derived from in-depth interviews recorded on audiotape for later transcription and analysis.

Keith's (1986) recommendation for approaching research tasks with the very old includes a research process conceptualized in three distinct stages. The three-stage model is adopted in the field to organize research tasks, and in this volume to organize reporting of the results. Each stage of the project has its own goals, activities, and resulting data. Stage One, the introductory phase, includes the tasks of preparation, gaining entry and acceptance, observation, and the recording of extensive fieldnotes. Stage Two involves developing focused research questions and conducting interviews designed to answer them. Stage Three is the analysis of the data collected in Stage Two, confirmation in the field of the results derived from the analysis, and the construction of reports clarifying the results. Stage

One is summarized in the next chapter, "A Day in the Nursing Home," a composite day of routine events in long-term care. But first, the procedures used in the field are noted in the remainder of this chapter.

The primary task at the outset of any research project is to assemble a set of research tools that will effectively permit the questions proposed to be addressed. In this study, the literature suggests five general areas that should be addressed. These five areas frame a protocol to guide the research process. Each of the five areas is addressed here.

First, evidence is sought to confirm the negative effects of high television use, which are said to include low self-esteem, irrational fears, depression, negative beliefs about aging, and social withdrawal. Since some of these factors may be associated with institutionalization, no conclusions can be drawn about high television use as a cause, but the co-occurrence of one or more of these negative views with particular media use patterns can be noted.

Second, the amount of television, the relation of television to other media, and the frequency and duration of media activities relative to other activities yield time-use data, which are essential to comparison with other subjects and with other populations in the evaluation of healthy and unhealthy media consumption and activity patterns.

Third, an unhealthy consumption style implies not only high levels of media use but also a pattern of nonselective media use. While a wide variety of use patterns would be anticipated overall, symptoms of nonselective media use include lack of variety in a media diet, inability to discriminate between choices, lack of preferences (not inability to express preferences), and inability to critically assess media content.

Fourth, content trends would indicate patterns of preference for certain programs, program types, genres, and styles. Elicited through documenting favorites, interviews can also reveal the sources of pleasure and the gratifications derived from media consumption.

Fifth, examination of patterns of social activity and the social uses of media among those who have successfully adapted to long-term care indicate the role and importance of media activities in a successful social transition.

Overall, the protocol is designed to elicit (1) the factors that contribute to heavy television viewing; (2) the degree of satisfaction derived from television viewing; (3) whether television in the nursing home is used as a substitute for other media, or to avoid contact, withdraw, or disengage socially; and (4) how television functions within the institutional regime and the daily schedule of residents.

Theoretically compatible with the goals of the project and with the particular needs of residents of long-term care, a social action perspective articulated by Anderson and Meyer (1988) examines media consumption as communication practices integrated with other areas of social life. Social action seeks to uncover the logical premises that guide action through eliciting verbal accounts that define action in the actors' own terms. Comparison of accounts reveals the sources of agreement and discord that are shared between individuals and among communities. Atchley (1989) argues that continuity, a key concept in studying activity participation, can only be studied with methods that utilize retrospection as well. Most important for this project, the standards of assessment reside within the constructs used by individuals to organize their own perceptions.

Perceptions of continuity, according to Atchley, are distilled and reformulated into themes that form the basis for identity. Therefore, in interview sessions, attention is paid to evidence of personal identity, including objects, activities, and preferences that reveal elements of self-definition. According to Atchley, identity is created in the present from reexamination of events and symbols from the past, using the continuity of the constructed life history to make sense and create a coherent story with plot, purpose, and the self as a central character.

New experiences are rarely totally unfamiliar. Atchley argues that new experiences tend to fall within an abstract domain of some area of proficiency, allowing the application of previously learned strategies, roles, and responses. Within this continuity framework, adjustment to a nursing home environment can be seen as a concrete set of tasks that stimulate efforts to find external continuity in a new environment. Thus, interviews focus on the continuity of life stories, the constructs used to organize perceptions, and self-definitions of the tasks of adjustment to the new environment in order to identify the logical premises that guide activity—in other words, how people define, explain, and rationalize their own actions.

Finally, the analysis is concerned with strategic manipulation of media, which is a resource-dependent communication model. Thus a Communication Resource Inventory (see Table 3.1) is compiled for each of the key resident informants, suggesting the resources available that can be manipulated toward accomplishing strategic ends.

The first stage of field research involves gaining entry and acceptance. Two criteria were initially used to establish a research site. First, the facility should have both residential and comprehensive levels of care present, ensuring a range of treatment situations and eliminating some attenuation due to changes in level of care over the course of the study. Second, the facility should meet federal guidelines and be certified to receive Medicare/Medicaid reimbursement. This ensures that the facility chosen would be expected to comply with federal standards that specify staff/patient ratios and basic equipment and service needs. The site chosen is in a midsized university city in central Indiana. Of the available sites, it has the broadest demographic range of residents who are not limited to a single background, religious group, or fraternal organization.

Hilltop (a pseudonym) is a medium-sized facility, housed in a relatively new building, on a rural site not far from the center of town. The residents initially encountered at Hilltop expressed active interest in assisting with this project, suggesting two additional qualifications: first, the basic daily needs of the residents were probably being met, which would allow them to consider the option of participation; and second, participant enthusiasm was judged to be an asset, considering that participation would require considerable cooperation, effort, and time commitment.

Hilltop is a comparatively large facility with 154 comprehensive beds and six residential units. Advertising a homelike atmosphere, the facility also offers a selective menu, laundry, beauty/barber services, ice cream parlor, gift shop, family and recreational lounge areas, and a regular schedule of activities publicized through the distribution of a monthly newsletter. Resident rooms are sparsely furnished, but residents are encouraged to personalize by augmenting the furnishings with a few of their own possessions.

Ethnographic Methodology

TABLE 3.1. Communication Resource Inventory

Communication Resource Inventory

Name_____

	low	medium	high

Tangible Possessions

    Money
    Property
    Technology
    Other_____

Communication Physiology

    Mobility
    Cognition
    Energy
    Unscheduled time
    Sight
    Hearing
    Speech
    Other_____

Skills/Knowledge

    Work/professional
    Hobbies
    Education
    Interests
    Other_____

Social Contacts

    Long-term friends
    Family members
    Caregiver relations
    Roommate relations
    Other_____

Comments:

Gaining initial acceptance means orienting to the space as well as its inhabitants. At the first stage an important task is to establish a basic map of the setting. Hilltop is shaped like a Christian cross with the longer of the four corridors containing the main entry from the parking lot, the administrative offices, dining room, concessions, and facility treatment rooms. The primary nursing station is located at the intersection of the four hallways, channeling all traffic through a central observation zone.

From the outset of the project it became apparent that status is clearly attached to the degree of each resident's independence. The geographical layout with its various units is an easily apprehended manifestation of this independence. Residential accommodations are more homelike, and skilled care is more hospital-like. The units reside on separate wings of the building, allowing level of care to take precedence over social considerations in placement decisions. The expectation for activity participation decreases as residents are moved from residential to intermediate or skilled care when greater medical intervention is deemed necessary. In skilled care, residents' medical needs are given priority over all other needs.

Overall, media use at Hilltop is complex and pervasive. All rooms have telephone and cable television access, but residents must supply their own television sets. Daily newspapers are available on a subscription basis or from on-site vending machines. A facility-owned television is kept "on" in the skilled care dining area during meals. There are books, magazines, and a television in each of the six public lounges. Television often runs all day in the activity room, a kitchen-like arts and crafts area where residents come to socialize or to work on specific projects. In addition to their televisions sets, most residents also have their own radios, books, and magazines. Any media product desired, such as a book or videotape, can be ordered by phone, carried in by family, or delivered by mail.

A number of the more prominent routine activities listed in the monthly event calendar are media centered. These include a weekly movie, a current events discussion group, and a reading group. With three full-time staff members in the activity department, residents rely on volunteer assistance for some of the regularly scheduled activities, including media events. In addition, spontaneous informal gatherings frequently arise, such as a group interested in following a particular news event. Groups of people gather regularly to watch soap operas, sporting events, and game shows as well. All of these contribute to the media-rich institutional environment.

With the goal of developing contacts into key informants, the first research task involves attending as many public events as possible in the hope of gaining trust. The theoretical goal at this point is also to identify significant events and themes in order to establish units of analysis on which to focus more directed inquiry later on. Beginning with media events in public areas, observation later evolves into participation in informal interaction. The primary research activity of the introductory phase is logging extensive fieldnotes that become a primary data source for the the project. Later an audio tape recorder is introduced to capture sustained conversations and interviews, but initial conversations are unstructured, friendly, and informal.

Initially, the media event serves as an observational unit of analysis, bracketed by the practices that participants adopt in organizing their own individual participation. Public media events are defined as events in which use of a communication medium is central to a scheduled activity. Scheduling means that the activity is planned in advance and published in the monthly calendar such that any of the residents might attend. The monthly activity calendar is an essential tool in determining what events are public, but is not the only factor ensuring participation. Attendance fluctuates relative to the time of day and the importance attached to the occasion. Some events attract a smaller and more specialized audience, while the more popular, public midday events attract as many as two-thirds of the resident population and many of the on-duty staff, with and without direct care responsibilities.

To illustrate the typical media event, consider a public gathering with consistently high attendance which is listed in the calendar as "Around the World." Scheduled for early afternoon, the event is meant to simulate a travel experience, focusing on the customs of a different culture each week. Participants gather in the main dining room and are entertained with music, decorations, food, a game or other activity, and travel films borrowed from a local travel agency. The event focusing on Hawaii, for example, centers around a film sponsored by Dole fruit growers. Setting the mood with paper flowers on each of the dining room tables, each participant is served a taste of crushed pineapple in a paper cup. Tapes of traditional Hawaiian music complete the mood and several members of the staff entertain the residents with their version of a hula dance, complete with grass skirts and paper leis. The activity director asks trivia questions and gives prizes, and people who have been to Hawaii are encouraged to talk about their experiences.

Some of the residents lead a fairly high-profile social life, attending public functions such as "Around the World," and spending much of their time in the lounges, hallways, and other public areas. These people prove easy to meet as they tend to introduce themselves and encourage association. Other residents tend to keep to their own rooms and venture out as little as possible. As with any group, there are some who are more gregarious and eager to meet strangers, while others seek more privacy. But over time, with residents introducing their friends, it became easier to meet and get to know many of the residents who would not have introduced themselves. Thus a strategy of networking is adopted where initial contacts are used to create links to other residents, creating a volunteer sample of maximum participation.

With the goal of meeting all the residents who came through the facility during the course of the fieldwork, introductions were sought with all residents who did not readily introduce themselves. Some were unable to converse, either being too ill or unresponsive to changes in the environment. In cases where resident introductions were not possible, some introduction was accomplished through the activity staff in daily rounds to deliver mail and chat with bedridden residents. Conversations with doctor, nurse, and family caregivers helped determine the strengths and weaknesses of residents in order to maximize the productivity of interview sessions. As anticipated, there were broad differences in the individual levels of involvement, capability, and interest in cooperating with the project. More than half of the residents were able to participate in conversations about their communication routines. Of this group, twenty-six of the residents were able to assist with formal interviews, which are summarized in the second stage of this report.

Out of the residents who graciously agreed to share their lives for this study, sustained inquiry was accomplished with a core group of nursing home residents whose lives provide much of the detail that illustrates this report. Many, of course, were capable of only a transient impact on the study. It was anticipated in a project of this scope that some residents would leave the facility, some would die, and others would become inaccessible for prolonged contact. However, the core group of residents each maintained a working relationship for more than a year within the course of this project. They participated in multiple interview sessions and revealed intimate details about their overall communication patterns, significant relationships, and everyday media consumption routines. In the latter stages of the interview process these key informants were also asked to confirm the conclusions drawn about their experiences.

The next chapter represents a summary of the findings from the first stage of the research. Field observations of the typical media-centered routines of nursing home residents introduce key resident informants and suggest some of the ways that daily media routines structure everyday institutional life.

Chapter 4

A Day in the Nursing Home

First impressions of the nursing home are likely to be colored heavily by one's prior experiences in medical contexts. Initial institutional assaults to the senses include antiseptic-tinged odors and equally unpleasant sounds emanating from darkened rooms. The code of dress signifies an easily apprehended medical hierarchy in the uniforms of professionals and workers that contrasts sharply with the slippers and pajamas worn by most of the residents. Moreover, the business complex with its parking facility, time clock, regimented meal times, and office appointment scheduling all provide additional cues that signify a busy medical facility with nearly as many employees as residents.

As the routines and the occupants of the facility become more familiar, however, it becomes apparent that residents see the nursing home quite differently than staff and outsiders see it. They come to consider the facility their home, and the impression is evident in the way they speak about it and move through it. Undertanding the significance of stressing the "home" in "nursing home" meant crossing a threshold that is both a literal invitation to entry and revelatory early moment.

Theoretical arguments are reintroduced in sections that follow, but first a description of some of the practices and routines involved in media consumption in the nursing home comprises this chapter. The "day" presented here is a composite day derived from many separate events in the first stage of research. While a composite day is fictive to the degree that this is not any particular calendar day, it is derived from actual experience. Observation conducted around the clock and interview sessions with residents and staff determine the events that are used here to typify each participant's daily routines.

The experiences are presented as a single day in order to convey some of the temporal sense of rhythm and flow that an actual day involves. This device is also useful to show how individual experience is related to and organized within the framework of an institutional schedule. Following the description of a composite day is a summary of some of the findings yielded from the first stage of the research.

4:00 a.m.

The only visible movement this early in the morning is at the brightly-lit nurses' station, standing as a hub for four dim corridors over which white-clad figures keep watch. The nurses occasionally venture out from behind the counter to where few sounds are audible aside from soft rubber-soled footsteps in one of the hallways and the metallic rasp of one errant wheel of the medicine cart being readied for morning rounds. Low moans issue from the resident room next to the nurses' station where a new admittance has been awake and in pain most of the night.

Bert, whose previous roommate died less than twenty-four hours ago, says he was kept awake much of the night by the pained noises from the new occupant of the other bed in his room. Bert by now has become accustomed to the routine of these disturbances. Although he did not get much sleep, it does not much interfere with his morning. As usual, he rises before the sun and pulls on a pair of sweatpants and well-worn leather slippers. Removing a cardigan sweater from the chair next to his bed, he slips it over his pajama top. Then, picking up a plastic drinking cup with a bent straw from his nightstand, he stiffly makes his way from his room to the lounge across the hall, stopping briefly to greet two uniformed women behind the counter at the nurses' station. Once in the lounge, he pauses long enough to turn on the television, and he takes his usual seat at a formica-topped, square table in front of the set.

Familiar with Bert's routine, a young nurse's aide, Chris, picks up a heavy, plastic key ring and follows him into the lounge, asking how he slept. While they talk, she opens one of the locked cupboards in the large entertainment center housing the television and she withdraws a plastic basket filled with Ziplock bags. She finds one with Bert's name on it and removes a disposable lighter and several cigarettes. A new policy adopted when a disoriented resident set fire to his room mandates that Chris give Bert only one cigarette and light it for him herself. Instead, she deposits all three cigarettes and the lighter on the table next to an ashtray with a masking tape label bearing Bert's name.

Since he had consulted his *TV Guide* the night before, Bert knows that a John Wayne western begins at 4:30 on AMC, his favorite cable movie network. Although he has turned the television on, he ignores it until then, exchanging familiar banter with Chris. She lingers, flirting with him a little in this idle time toward the end of her shift.

Bert watches most of the early morning movie alone, with only a few interruptions. A nurse brings him juice and a small plastic cup containing his morning medications, and later two others drop in just to say hello. By the time the film is nearing its end, a number of other residents have risen. Only one other resident, however, named Dan, leaves his room to come to the lounge. He chats amiably with Bert, but stays only long enough to smoke his cigarette before turning back down the hall to his room.

With his movie over, lights on in the hallways, and activity beginning in the other resident rooms, Bert returns across the hall to his own room. Tuning his own television set to a morning news program, he changes his clothes and cleans up for breakfast. A few minutes after 7:00, he turns off his set and begins the slow walk past the nurses' station, down another corridor to the dining room where breakfast will be served at 7:30.

7:00 a.m.

Margaret has been awake for at least an hour with her television tuned to CNN, the cable news network, from the minute she opened her eyes. Although she has spent the last thirty minutes in the bathroom, she leaves the television set on, saying it serves as a sign to the nurses that she does not need to be wakened this morning. She is not supposed to use the toilet without assistance, but by the time the aide arrives to answer her call for help, Margaret has finished in the lavatory, even having time to wash up and comb her hair. The aide smiles while admonishing Margaret for her independence. Performing the only job left, she helps Margaret back into her wheelchair and hovers while Margaret wheels herself toward the bed.

Margaret's roommate, Lillian, is awake by this time. While checking the half-filled reservoir for her urinary catheter, the aide asks if she would like some assistance. As the aide tends to Lillian, Margaret wheels over to open the curtains on the large picture window that takes up most of the outside wall. The three women discuss the day's weather, with Margaret offering storm information from the morning TV news. The younger woman adds observations made during her early morning drive to work.

While engaged in the conversation Margaret moves around the bed. She straightens the barely disturbed covers and glances frequently at the news broadcast. She interrupts the conversation to draw attention to the television news broadcast that reports flooding in the Mississippi Valley. Margaret uses this story to reminisce about a flood she witnessed in Louisville. She thinks it was 1935, and Lillian, too, remembers the event well.

The aide brings Lillian a washbasin and towel from the bathroom, waiting while she washes her face. When the breakfast cart arrives from the kitchen, Lillian sits up in bed to eat her tea and toast, a position that enables her to see Margaret's television. Margaret sits in her wheelchair, careful not to obscure Lillian's view. They talk little while they eat. Lillian has difficulty maintaining a seated position for long periods of time. Margaret's arthritis-gnarled hands have difficulty grasping utensils, requiring much of her concentration. Their attention seems focused on the news broadcast which Margaret changes to the local station, a CBS affiliate, when she notices that the stories are repeating from the previous hour.

By 8:00 a.m., both women have pushed away their trays. Lillian lowers her bed to a more comfortable reclining position. Margaret dozes in her wheelchair, her head falling forward onto her chest. When someone comes to gather the breakfast trays, Margaret opens her eyes and asks for help getting back up onto the bed. Removing the remains of yesterday's newspaper from the nightstand, she spends the next hour combing it thoroughly, reading everything but the sports section and the classified ads, she says. Although her family brings in the day's paper in the afternoon, Margaret prefers to save it for the next morning.

At 9:00, a nurse comes to take Lillian to physical therapy, which wakes Margaret from a second doze. Pushing yesterday's paper into the trash, she reaches into a shopping bag next to her bed for a new Harlequin romance novel. Margaret reads two or three of these books each day. She will finish this one after lunch and then deposit the book into another paper bag that will be taken home when someone comes to visit in the afternoon.

10:00 a.m.

Bea and Barbara, two women in their late sixties, arrive separately in the activity room at about the same time. Barbara uses a wheelchair, like most of the residents, and Bea comes on foot. The activity director, Sharon, is just putting away boxes of nail polish and manicure instruments. Her assistant, Diane, is filling out the paperwork that documents which residents participated in this week's manicure sessions. Barbara says hello and goes directly to the television set, tuning it to the local station. Bea takes a seat near Barbara at a round table in front of the television next to another woman who is carefully turning pages in a magazine and chatting with Sharon while waiting for her nails to dry.

Like most of the residents, Barbara has her own television set in her room, but she comes to watch television in the activity room because she says she needs to "get out." Barbara doesn't get along that well with her roommate, who, she says, is exhibiting increasingly disturbing signs of dementia. She gets together with others in the activity room, which resembles a large kitchen with its stove and refrigerator, countertops and cupboards, two tables, shelves full of house plants, and a television set. Barbara watches her favorite game show and soap opera on the activity room television set, whether others watch with her or not. However, Bea can be found there most mornings, chatting with Barbara during the commercial breaks and before and after the programs.

As noon approaches, the slow-moving traffic of walkers and wheelchairs outside the activity room door increases as residents inch their way to the main dining room next door. When the program ends, Barbara turns off the television set. She and Bea set out from the activity room to join the others at their regular table for lunch.

1:00 p.m.

Clark sits with his friends, Bert and Charlie, and the newcomer, Ralph, at one of the cloth-covered square tables in the dining room where lunch is served. The high-ceilinged room is noticeably quiet, considering more than eighty people are seated here in groups of four. The men linger for a while after the meal, as they have each day for several years. They sit together talking, laughing, and teasing the teenage girl who works in the kitchen that comes to clear the tables. Mealtime is their primary activity together. Except for an occasional game of euchre in the evenings or ball game on television, the men rarely see each other outside of the dining room.

Mealtimes are major events that constitute a minimum of six hours per day. Mealtime includes the time for washing and dressing, traveling to and from the dining room, waiting to be served, and lingering afterward. Some residents who rely on others to wheel them to and from the dining room must wait at their tables for as much as an hour before and after the meal, but Clark and his friends take pride in the fact that they propel themselves. However, Ralph, the eldest and frailest of the four, moves so slowly that he usually accepts help when it is offered.

When the men break up their lunch meeting at about 1:15, each man takes off at his own speed, two of them on foot and two in wheelchairs. Clark begins the trek across the length of the dining room and down two corridors, a trip that usually takes him twenty-five minutes. Diane, the activity assistant, greets him as he exits the dining room. As they are going in the same direction, she asks Clark if he would like a push. He politely declines, saying that he needs the exercise. If he does not push himself down to the dining room, he says, he will not be hungry, and if he does not push himself back, he will not digest. She reminds him of the afternoon's bingo game at 2:30 in the dining room, offering to come get him. He declines the invitation, saying he does not think he is up to it today.

Returning to his room, Clark finds his roommate, Charlie, seated in the easy chair in front of his television set, which is tuned to the cable sports network, ESPN, for afternoon baseball. Wheeling between Charlie and the game on the way to his bed at the far side of the room, Clark pauses long enough to turn up the volume. Charlie cannot hear the television well, so to avoid disturbing others he keeps the volume all the way down when Clark is not there to advise him.

Pulling himself up onto his bed, Clark asks Charlie about the score. They talk briefly about the game and the two teams that are playing before they both doze off in front of the game. Clark wakes up again at about 3:00. He hears Charlie moving about, getting his coat from the closet for an afternoon walk. After Charlie leaves, Clark spends the next hour looking over his mail, which was delivered while he slept. Today he finds a *Reader's Digest*, one of the three magazines he subscribes to, and he spends a quiet hour with it alone.

3:30 p.m.

Diane, the activity assistant, pushes a wheelchair down the hall from the dining room, cheerfully agreeing with everything said by Adelle. The small woman seated in the chair does not recognize the corridor she is in today even though she has traveled this route hundreds of times. Nearing the nurses' station, Diane tries to maintain her smile and not wrinkle her nose, but the smell of urine grows stronger as she approaches the line of wheelchairs facing the long counter. Adelle begins pleading, "Please take me home" over and over. Diane tells her that she will be just fine right here, parking the chair at the end of the row.

One by one, three nurse's aides pluck the chairs from the end of the line, pushing the occupants to their rooms for changing and cleaning, until it is Adelle's turn. Nancy, the young woman pushing her chair, asks Adelle if she has to "go." Adelle does not answer the question, responding instead that it must be time to start dinner as her husband will be home soon. Relieved that Adelle has not soiled her clothes, Nancy waits until her charge finishes in the bathroom, then helps her back to her chair. After the fourth request for the time, Nancy stops providing an answer. Pushing the wheelchair back down the hallway, Adelle is returned to a place in the line across from the nurses' station. When Adelle, in an increasingly agitated tone, continues to insist that it must be time to start dinner, the aide checks her chart to see if it is time for Adelle's medication. Finding it is not, she wheels Adelle into the smoking lounge and places her next to a woman in a stained pink robe, who is seated in front of the television, staring with glazed eyes at the cartoons on the flickering screen.

4:30 p.m.

After returning to her room from the weekly bingo game in the dining room, Estelle turns on a lamp to light her side of the room and put away her winnings—two boxes of raisins and a granola bar—in her new but nearly empty miniature refrigerator. She's proud of the new appliance, which she acquired through her niece when her doctor prescribed a can of beer for her to drink each evening. Straightening the framed photographs on her dresser, she turns on the television set to check the only two channels she ever seems to watch: the local commercial CBS station, and TNN, The Nashville Network. Having missed all of her soap operas, she promptly changes channels from the local station that is rerunning the *Oprah Winfrey Show* to the country music videos being shown on TNN. She adjusts the volume until it is barely audible so as not to disturb her sleeping roommate.

Taking a tissue from the box next to her bed, she methodically begins dusting the things on her side of the room—first the television, then the bedside table, and then the pictures and knickknacks on her dresser. Although the housekeeping staff regularly dusts the furniture, she complains that they do not dust her personal things which, according to Estelle, is just as well. They are not as careful as she is with them. She has only a few possessions, but each item has its own significance. She dusts and rearranges them daily, especially the things displayed on the built-in shelf behind her television. Crowded together there are mementos and seasonal decorations. Among them are a popsicle stick ornament made by visiting school children, a homemade valentine from a friend's child, a small ceramic pumpkin filled with lollipops, pamphlets from various religious organizations that visit the nursing home, and a stuffed dog signed by the staff, a souvenir from her last trip to the hospital.

Satisfied with the results of her housekeeping, she combs her hair and adjusts her jewelry, moving a Christmas tree pin from the left shoulder of her flowered dress to the right. Putting away a string of pink plastic beads, she changes to the blue ones instead. When she finishes these tasks, Estelle settles on the bed with the midsection of the newspaper. She has the paper delivered each day. Although it arrives early in the morning while she is at breakfast, it takes all day for her to finish reading it because of her vision. She had a left cataract removed in an outpatient visit to the doctor a few weeks ago, and the right eye is yet to be done. So Estelle reads the news in the morning, saving what she calls the "women's page" for afternoon, and the comics and advertisements, if she gets to them, for after dinner in the evening.

When the program ends, Estelle takes this as a cue to turn off the television and start toward the dining room for the evening meal. She pauses for a moment to wait for Eileen, who lives across the hall. Although they sit at different tables, Estelle and Eileen travel at about the same rate. Leaving their rooms at about the same time, they often go down to the dining room together. They will return to their rooms just before 7:00, and Estelle will turn on television game shows and continue with her newspaper until it is time to get ready for bed at 8:00. Then, the nurse will come in with medication to help her sleep. Estelle keeps the television on most of the time when she is in her room. It is the first TV she has ever owned, a gift from her niece, and she loves it. In addition to the entertainment it provides, she says it also helps to block out the sounds coming from other rooms—most of them unpleasant. She continues to have the television on, hoping for religious programming, but watches whatever comes on The Nashville Network until 10:00. At that point, she turns it off to sleep.

6:00 p.m.

As Eileen is finishing her dinner in the dining room, she is approached by Angie, one of the activity assistants, who asks if she is coming to Current Events at 7:30 tonight. Eileen laughs, saying she will if she hasn't got a better offer. No one else at her table commits. Flo stares straight ahead, seeming not to hear, and Barbara says she will be asleep by 8:00. Bea has already gone back to her room. Eileen stands up, saying goodnight to her dinner companions. She pushes her own empty wheelchair back to her room. Maneuvering slowly through the crowded dining room, Eileen has to stop frequently in the crush of wheelchairs all headed through the dining room doorway at the same time. Seeming not to mind the delay, Eileen greets many of the others by name while waiting patiently for her opportunity to move out.

Returning to her room briefly, Eileen checks her reflection in the bathroom mirror, patting the blue-tinted curls she had done at the beauty shop that morning. After rinsing her mouth, she turns out the lights and sets out for the lounge where "Current Events" will be held.

When she arrives, just before 7:30, she finds six others. They are already sitting in darkness with the window shades drawn against the sunset. The television is on. Behind her Angie arrives pushing another resident. As her chair moves more slowly on the carpeting, Eileen allows Angie to push her chair into position, lining it up with the others in a semicircle around the television set. Changing the television channel from *Wheel of Fortune* to *Current Affair*, Angie signals she is about to begin. After adjusting the volume so all can hear it, Angie begins distributing paper bags of popcorn and trays of potato chips. Eileen is the only one who refuses them, saying she is unable to eat either one.

Eileen and the others watch the program, making occasional comments, while Angie peruses *USA Today*, hastily marking items of potential interest. When the program ends, she apologizes that the *Time/Life* film they normally use for Current Events did not arrive this week. She begins asking questions to provoke discussion, particularly over a program segment about new exercise equipment. None of the stories they saw this week had been particularly news-oriented, so Angie has difficulty starting discussion. Most of the participants either read the newspaper, watch TV news, or both. Discussions at this event focus on issues the group has some familiarity with, but Angie has trouble asking questions that connect this program to the group's experiences. Irma makes a comment related to exercise. Then she begins rambling in reminiscence about her childhood. The group members begin to show signs that they have lost interest in group discussion tonight, moving around and talking among themselves. Bob excuses himself and Eileen moves her chair aside so that he can get out. Interrupting Irma's story, Angie makes a last attempt at control, asking Eileen whether she exercised when she was young. Eileen answers brusquely that running a business and raising children was exercise enough. Her comment, that no one that she knew had time or money for exercise equipment and lessons on how to use it, served to bring the discussion to an abrupt close.

Angie raises her voice in one last gesture to regain control and announces tomorrow's activity department events while people begin to move out. Then she turns on the overhead lights for people to leave. As Eileen is seated near the door, she is one of the first to depart, keeping near the rail at the side of the hallway so she can support herself now and then. Angie passes her several times as she delivers other residents back to their rooms.

Eileen pants a little from the effort as she enters her room. Seeing that her roommate, Alice, is asleep already, she pulls the curtain separating the two beds, puts on her nightgown, and pulls herself up onto her bed. Turning on the table lamp and the television set, she looks at TV for a while, but she cannot figure out which program she is watching.

The nurse comes in just before 9:00 to bring Eileen some juice and a cracker with her pills. Before she leaves, Eileen asks her to turn the channel to try to find some news, explaining that her hands do not work well enough to operate the channel selector since her last stroke about a year ago. Because changing channels is a difficult task for her, she claims to know little about the broadcast schedule. Sitting on the bed, the younger woman consults Alice's *TV Guide* and says that there is no news broadcast scheduled until 10:00. Thanking her just the same, Eileen says she thinks she will not be awake that long. However, when the channel that is on happens to begin a special on the conflict in the Middle East, she smiles and says that this is just what she wanted. When asked if she did not already get enough news at Current Events that night, Eileen replies that the group never seems to talk about the day's news; they only talk about events from the past.

Saying good night to the nurse, Eileen drinks her juice and watches the special for a while, falling asleep by about 9:30. When the nurse makes her rounds a little after 10:00, she turns off Eileen's lamp and the television set and opens the curtain between the two beds.

10:00 p.m.

As the credits for the CBS series *Matlock* roll, Gerry points the remote control at the set, changing the channel to VH-1, the adult-contemporary cable music video station. Gerry's husband, Dan, swings his legs over the side of the bed and balances on his feet just long enough to grip the handlebars of his motorized scooter. Negotiating a tight turn next to his bed, he heads the small electric vehicle out of the room, leaving the door open behind him.

Hearing the low hum of the motor as he approaches the nurses' station, Peg, the registered nurse on duty, heads for their room to tend to Gerry. Pam, one of the aides on duty, picks up the key ring to get Dan his last cigarette of the night. Knowing that Peg will be busy with Gerry for at least fifteen minutes, Pam unlocks a second cupboard and removes her oversized purse. She decides to take her break with Dan, but sits in the doorway, so she will know if a resident signals for help on the electronic callboard. Taking two videotapes out of her bag, she gives them to Dan, telling him that she and her boyfriend liked one and did not care for the other. After examining the titles, Dan tells her the one she and her boyfriend did not like is one that he and Gerry have already seen, but he has not heard of the other. The second tape is directed by Clint Eastwood, she says, knowing that Dan likes his films.

When he sees Peg coming back down the hall, Dan leaves the smoking lounge, saying good night to Pam. Thanking her for the tape, he tells her he will return it to her tomorrow. Halfway down the hall, Dan meets the nurse, and she asks him if Gerry has been sleeping well lately. They discuss her trip to the doctor next week, speculating that the doctor will alter her medication.

When Dan returns to their room, he closes the door, first making certain the hand-lettered "Knock Before Entering" sign is in place. Finding her in a clean nightgown with clean sheets on both of their pushed-together hospital beds, he asks her preference in snack foods. Dan hands the borrowed videotape to Gerry, asking if she has heard of the title. He then starts preparing a snack—a large bowl of popcorn made in their electric popper, and two cans of fruit juice from the small refrigerator standing in the corner of the room. They are lucky to have both appliances, Gerry says, as they had to get special permission to have a refrigerator in their room. The corn popper was a wedding gift they got five years ago when they got married in the nursing facilty. When the popcorn is ready, Dan runs his scooter over to the VCR at the foot of the beds to put in the tape. Before starting the machine, he changes into his pajamas, visits the bathroom, and adjusts the lighting. Climbing back into bed with two remote controls, they settle down to watch the film.

Less than an hour into the film, they are both bored with it, and Dan stops the tape. He gets up out of bed and puts the tape back in its case, placing it in the bag on the back of his scooter. Opening the folding door to their closet, he takes out a cardboard box holding thirty or more videotapes. Removing a comedy, *Turner and Hootch*, that they have watched several times already, he places it in the VCR and starts the tape.

Gerry falls asleep before the movie has ended. As soon as Dan notices she is asleep, he stops the tape. Then rewinds it a bit, guessing where she dozed off. Leaving the tape in the machine, he turns it off so they can pick it up from there tomorrow. Dan watches a bit of *The Tonight Show*, but is not too fond of Jay Leno. He soon turns off the television and the lights, and turns on the radio, tuning in a jazz program. He listens until he falls asleep at about 1:00 a.m., waking up again at 6:00 when he goes to the smoking lounge for a cigarette with Bert while the morning nurse comes in to tend to Gerry.

SUMMARY OF STAGE ONE

Preparation to move into the second stage of research involves analysis of these initial observations, represented here in the description of media routines that occur in a typical day at Hilltop. The description portrays media events as embedded in the everyday social routines of interactants.

Bert's early morning movie routine is entwined with his smoking ritual, avoidance of his new roommate, and socializing with the nurses and his friend Dan. Margaret's early morning news routine serves as a sign of her competence, that she is up and taking care of herself. Not only does television encompass her personal care rituals, it accommodates her breakfast routine with her roommate Lillian, which might otherwise be conducted in awkward silence. And television affords them both an opportunity to reminisce about common events in their separate pasts.

For Bea and Barbara, the television in the activity room provides a place for them to socialize with a routine that simulates a housewives' coffee klatch. Like Bert, Barbara and her roommate do not get along, but the activity lounge provides an alternate space to meet, and the television that accompanies the visit functions to facilitate their socialization, with both structural and relational dimensions. Similarly, Clark and Charlie spend their afternoons in a routine of sports television that accommodates sports talk, reading, and an afternoon nap. It should be noted that both pairs adopt routines that are gender inflected as well. Their television choices are among the few opportunities available within the homogenizing institutional setting for residents to express a gendered self.

For Adelle, entering the latter stages of dementia, the television provides a focal point for her attention, while marking the stratification of the institution according to pervasive but sometimes subtle perceptions of mental competency. Television serves to accommodate the nursing staff routines as well, distracting Adelle from a nearly constant state of worry. In the afternoon, program choice in the lounge is controlled by the nurses, who believe the color cartoons are visually stimulating to Adelle and her peers. The cartoons also provide an unambiguous sign to others that the lounge is undesirable until Adelle and her company return to their rooms.

For Estelle, the television in her room is both object and structural presence as it accommodates her housekeeping rituals and her newspaper routines. Television marks time for meals and for other activities, and her program choices are highly ritualized in a daily routine that seems to pay little regard to the topical content of the programs. In contrast, Eileen uses the television primarily as an information tool, serving to keep her in touch with local and world events. Just as important as a window on the world, it serves also as a sign to others of her interest in world events.

From the 4:00 a.m. interaction between Bert and the nurses who tend to his needs to the late-night routines of Dan and Gerry, it is apparent that media use at Hilltop is intertwined with events and routines that contribute to their meaning. Above all, the relationships maintained in the facility indicate the styles of media consumption adopted by residents. Personal relationships observed at this stage are of four types: roommate pairs, family members, patient/staff relations, and friendships. Questions designed to reveal the impact of these relationships are pursued in the interviews conducted in the second stage of research.

In addition to relationship influences, media routines reflect the influences of the physical constraints and the varying abilities of nursing home residents, and the everyday institutional demands with which they live. Further, the degree to which media routines reflect continuity or depart from past consumption patterns is also probed at the next stage. Where changes in routines are evident, questions are asked about the nature and reasons for adaptations.

Finally, media content choices themselves appear to be quite diverse. Print choices include a variety of newpapers, magazines, and paperback books. Television choices also appear to encompass every available content genre, and observations reveal remarkably few common elements. Questions that probe choice making attempt to reveal other patterns in style, pleasure, and gratification that transcend media genre as an explanatory mechanism. Each of these issues is taken up following a description of the goals, activities, and data yielded in the next stage of research.

STAGE TWO: NARROWING THE FOCUS

The second stage of the research project involves entering the site for a period of more focused research. The goals at this stage shift from a more generalized mapping to the investigation of specific questions. The primary activity at the second stage is establishing productive interview relationships, in contrast with the more casual, conversational relations of the first stage cultivated primarily to build trust. From an initial pool of seventy-seven volunteers, the data yielded at the second stage are derived from completed interview responses accomplished with twenty-six Hilltop residents. Although this seems on the surface like very low levels of completion, considering the frailty and unstable health of many of the residents, it is not. Multiple interview sessions necessary to describe the entire media environment were possible with about a third of them. Examination of the partial interview responses, however, indicate no significant systematic deviation from completed interviews.

The basic interview protocol covers three broad areas: biographical, current preferences and patterns, and past media preferences and patterns. The biographical information recorded includes age, sex, ethnic background, family information, nursing home tenure, former lifestyle and occupation, current source of income, and current visitors. Current and past media patterns are explored with questions focused on each communication medium, looking for information about taste preferences and uses of media. The interviews concentrate on detail, using specific questions about how residents spend their time, what activities are engaged in for pleasure, and what personal preferences and practices constitute the media environment as a whole. An important analytic goal is to identify common experiences and factors related to the enjoyment of activities. Although the specific questions differ from one interview to another, probes are designed to elicit as much information as possible about favorite pastimes and pleasures, while allowing for maximum reflection and unhurried storytelling.

Reduction of the interview responses begins with broad categorical areas such as preferences for a particular medium, genre, or program. Regularities are noted that contribute to the creation of a common media background or experience. Refinement of these concepts leads to the development of "disciplined abstractions" (Lofland, 1976). Interviews progress toward focus on the the individual motivations and satisfactions that comprise the media consumption experience. Anticipating that certain institutional policies and individual physical limitations would also exert their influence, questions focus not only on present media routines but also probe the adaptation of long-standing life patterns.

Chapter 5

Program Preferences and Routines

A survey of the media preferences of nursing home residents reflects a variety of tastes, experiences, and habits of individuals who use unique strategies to adapt to their present circumstances. But while each person's tastes are highly individualized, Hilltop residents also respond to shared institutional demands and expectations. For the insight they provide into the common elements of the experience, notable regularities are discussed here, organized according to some of the recurrent themes that arise in interview responses.

Although Hilltop provides a variety of reading materials, including books, magazines, and newspapers that are readily available to those who want them, overall reading levels at Hilltop remain low, particularly in relation to the time spent in television consumption. For the most avid readers, the time spent reading amounts to a little more than four hours per day. But even for avid readers, page volume remains comparatively low, averaging less than fifty pages per day. Residents read only one local newspaper, but the range of magazines is more varied, with no universal favorite choices. Hobby magazines, news magazines, and women's magazines are favorite types, with *TV Guide, Ladies Home Journal,* and *Readers' Digest* the only titles mentioned by multiple residents.

Hilltop residents have cable access to more than thirty different television channels at any given time. With an availability that many older people in independent living situations do not share, it renders television additionally attractive and the most popular medium in the facility. Consumption totals average more than ten hours per day for this small sample. And if the actual hours of sets turned on were calculated without regard to usage—that is, not counted during significant attention lapses such as sleep—the average would be much higher than ten hours per day. Some residents report leaving the television running sixteen to twenty hours per day. The night nursing staff count turning off television sets among the routine tasks of their nightly rounds, beginning just before midnight.

Favorite television channels also vary by individual taste, but the three major networks (ABC, CBS, and NBC), Public Television, the cable channels CNN (Cable News Network), AMC (American Movie Classics), the Weather Channel, and A&E (Arts and Entertainment) are common favorites. The interviews also reveal a strong preference for the local CBS network affiliate television station, the local channel that originates in the same town as the nursing home, and the only channel mentioned universally by all the interviewees. Ninety percent (twenty-three) say they regularly watch the local news, and 77 percent (twenty) report regularly watching other programming on the same local station.

There is an array of individual favorites airing on the local channel, but of particular shared interest are the evening game shows. After the evening meal on any given day, a walk through the corridors of Hilltop finds a majority of television sets tuned to *Wheel of Fortune* and *Jeopardy*. The *Lawrence Welk* program rerun on Public Television is the only other program title mentioned by a majority. Other evening favorites mentioned frequently are *Highway to Heaven, Murder She Wrote,* and *Barnaby Jones* reruns. Prime-time programs mentioned cross all program genres, including situation comedy, drama, mysteries, and news magazines, but more than a third of the programs mentioned are carried on the local CBS affiliate. About half of the women routinely watch soap operas in the afternoon. Of those who do, there is a clear preference for the soaps aired on the local CBS affiliate as well, over the other available options.

The preference for the local television station might best be explained as local habit developed over time, reflecting a recent past before widespread use of cable television when there was a limited number of channel choices. Habituation to program favorites such as the local news and the soap operas, then, would be most comprehensible from this perspective. However, it would not explain the clear affinity for prime-time programming on the local channel. With a rapidly changing television milieu that yields a new programming schedule each season, preference for local evening broadcasts in prime time suggests that there are other factors at work as well, factors that include technophobia as well as habituation.

Some residents cite local weather information as a reason to prefer the local station, knowing that storm sightings will interrupt the program if necessary. However, any of the half-dozen stations originating within the state provide basically the same service. And cable television's weather channel provides a constant source of information about the climate. Rather, the preference for local television seems to encompass a larger sense of desire for community affiliation, and a desire to stay in touch with local affairs. Probing the reasons for this preference, residents also say they enjoy the advertisements from local businesses, and they have a preference for familiar local television personalities. They especially like catching a glimpse of local landmarks and staying informed about special local events.

The interest in local channels for information extends to print media as well, with 50 percent (thirteen) reporting that they read the local newspaper regularly. Another 38 percent (ten) say they stopped subscribing to the newspaper only recently while in the facility. They cite two factors prohibiting newspaper use: the cost of subscription and deteriorating vision. Eileen talks about the importance of local information for her, saying that news keeps her in touch with the community:

> I like the news more than anything. The current, local news. You have to keep up and know what's going on. Even though you can't be with it, you keep up with things. I like to read my paper for that too. I keep up with the news all the time.

And Bert has this comment:

> I like to watch the news to keep up on what's going on. Things happen so fast anymore you can't hardly keep up. And I used to take the paper every day, but no more. It's too rich for me now. I read the paper. Sometimes. When I get it. But if I had to pay for it, I wouldn't have it at all.

Those who do read the newspaper every day say it takes longer than it used to, but most feel that it is worth the effort invested.

Despite interruptions, they return to the task, often taking three to four hours each day to complete a single edition of the newspaper. One lengthy reading session is uncommon, however, and more likely the newspaper is consumed in two or more sessions spread out over the day.

The importance of the act of reading the daily newspaper is enhanced when examined in terms of reading levels in general, which are comparatively low. Although some avid readers in the facility did not choose to participate in this study, overall the survey is skewed toward the inclusion of the more alert and articulate residents. While 77 percent (twenty) report that they regularly read one or more magazines, 27 percent (seven) read *TV Guide* only. Also 23 percent (six) still read books, but all of this group say that they have difficulty completing a novel. They cite four factors that inhibit book reading: problems with vision, the inability to concentrate, frequent interruptions, and the tendency to fall asleep. Those who do read books tend to read formulaic westerns and romances, or they reread familiar favorites. Yet, for some, a pattern of nonreading does not represent change and is consistent with their earlier lives. Eileen says this:

> I read some, but I go to sleep if I read too much. There's several books I've read. But I wasn't ever a big reader like some of them. Articles or short stories, that's what I like. Because [if] I lay one [a book] down, I never get back to it.

But for others like Gerry, nonreading represents a loss:

> I just can't read anymore. My eyes just won't cooperate with me. And I miss it, sure.

As the preceding comments suggest, news is an important content genre for Hilltop residents, who cite the desire to stay in touch with the community as an important factor in news consumption. But entertainment program tastes are evident as well. Game shows, soap operas, movies, and situation comedies are ranked highly among different Hilltop residents. These choices are limited only by an individual's ability to enjoy his or her favorites, a topic taken up in the next section. And the movement from newspapers to television news, while not universal, is noteworthy. The adaptation is necessitated by constraints, physical limitations, and financial limitations. This leads residents to seek out alternate channels to maintain consistency with past preferences and tastes.

But the trend in preferences that most strongly illustrates adaptation is in the area of music. Residents only rarely listen to the radio, and very few have their own recordings. Despite these factors, interest in some form of music remains high, with a number citing musical television formats among their favorites, emphasizing that continuity with preferences and practices developed early in life is subject to the availability of a medium to satisfy those desires.

Previous research indicates a decline in interest in popular music among the aged (Chaffee and Wilson, 1975), although Bliese (1982) reports that 62 percent of her sample still enjoy listening to tapes and phonograph records occasionally. At Hilltop use of recordings is low, with only 8 percent (two) saying they listen to tapes once in a while. Recordings do not appear to be seen as much of a loss, however, because this particular group say they never invested much in recorded music. Events such as the Great Depression of the 1930s and World War II inhibited purchase, and any they once owned are now gone. The two who do currently listen to tapes both acquired cassette machines and recorded music within the last few years.

In the course of their lives, this group says they spent more time listening to the radio for music than to recordings, and 35 percent (nine) say that they still listen to the radio for both news and music on occasion. But for the rest the radio is not a good source anymore. They attribute the drop in radio consumption to two factors, changes in contemporary radio formats and difficulty with hearing. However, 65 percent (seventeen) indicate strong preferences continue for music on television, citing country western and gospel formats as among their favorites.

Music television includes cable music stations (MTV, VH-1, TNN) which hold only a little interest for this group, but a particular Hilltop favorite is the previously mentioned *Lawrence Welk* hour, which reruns on the public television station twice on Saturday and on Sunday evenings. This show is watched by more than half of the Hilltop residents in any given week. Others say that they look forward to special musical presentations such as Handel's *Messiah* or other holiday music specials. Also regular, weekly programs with a strong musical component like the religious program *700 Club*, or variety shows and live concerts are typical favorites.

In addition to the 54 percent (fourteen) who say they regularly watch movies on television, another 38 percent (ten) say they only turn on a movie if it is a musical. *The Sound of Music* was volunteered by half (five) of these as their all-time favorite film. Older films are universally preferable to new movies, which is partially due to the difficulty devoting two uninterrupted hours to a single activity.

Taken together, these figures suggest a desire to continue to appreciate music through the medium that is most available, television. Estelle says:

> I like to play them [audio cassettes] when I'm alone. Also radios and what have you, the hi-fi music [vinyl records]. And, well, television I like the same way. Only you don't hear that coming out the window.

Hearing loss renders listening alone a less attractive option. But with television, as Estelle indicates, music can be enjoyed at a lower volume, that will not "come out the window" with the addition of the visual element.

Although radio use has declined, they fondly remember the radio era from beginning to end. Big band musicians, live country music radio programs, and the *Hit Parade* are all mentioned as former favorites. But the medium that makes these forms available now is television. The cable television channel AMC (American Movie Classics) is mentioned by several as a particular favorite source for musical television.

The shifts from newspaper consumption to television news, and from radio and recordings to music television sources, support the concept of substitution formulated by Bliese (1982) and others (Danowski, 1975; Kubey, 1980). But while television appears to be used as a substitute for other media, and as a substitute for firsthand information about the local community, results do not support a conclusion that it is used as a substitute for companionship.

Rather, the interview sessions suggest a strong association between the amount of television consumed and satisfaction with one's roommate. Roommate satisfaction is most evident in descriptions of the evening consumption routines. Although Hilltop residents go to sleep comparatively early—the facility is quiet by 9:00 p.m.—81 percent (twenty-one) say they watch some television in the evenings. All of the interviewees, whether they spend their evenings with television or not, say that evening is the most pleasurable time of day for television. They cite four factors contributing to its pleasure: better programming, no interference from scheduled obligations, less noise in the facility, and the ability to relax more completely.

Those who do not consume television in the evenings also express greater dissatisfaction with nursing home life. Since evening is so unanimously considered the most pleasurable time for television at Hilltop (as, perhaps, elsewhere as well) the circumstances surrounding the exercise of that particular pleasure and the factors that might be considered inhibitors are probed more deeply. The connection between television, roommates, and satisfaction is explored in interview sessions conducted in the evenings with roommate pairs who both do and do not use television at that time.

Furthermore, of those who report recent changes in their patterns of television consumption or dissatisfaction with their present routines, conflict with roommates is cited as the most frequent reason for dissatisfaction. Roommate conflicts that interfere with evening television consumption include complaints from roommates who cannot sleep while the other's television is on, differences in program tastes where the roommate's choice prevails, and roommates who make too much noise, either from pain and discomfort or from their own television sets, to render listening and concentration possible. The next chapter looks more closely at roommate pairs for further insight into the roommate relationship and the domestic patterns of media use in long-term care.

Chapter 6

Roommates and Coordination

Making a successful adjustment to nursing home life is an achievement of stability, however one measures such accomplishments. While the notion of what constitutes successful adjustment is not easily measured, as Bettinghaus and Bettinghaus (1976) have demonstrated, tenure is one indicator of success in adaptation to the new social system. At Hilltop, passing a year in long-term care is considered an achievement that yields more than one measure of stability. At a year's time, more or less, long-term care residents will have achieved stable routines in caretaking and domestic relations, characterized by an ability to predict and exert some control over some everyday activities.

Further than that, a few are able to achieve highly coordinated domestic routines that can be seen as successful management of domesticity. Such routines include taking turns with the bathroom, coordinating naps, and the adoption of coordinated media routines such as reading time and shared radio or television programs. Relationships at this level of function should be seen as too ambitious for all that enter a nursing home, and they are especially ambitious for those that enter under traumatic conditions. But each person who does enter nursing care deserves and appreciates the small achievements of domestic satisfaction. Those who are capable of settling into everyday routines of domesticity express pleasure at being able to do so. Television, counted among the domestic routines, is frequently grouped with other pleasurable sources of sensual stimulations in interview responses.

The pleasures result from small, private routines. But there is common resonance in the responses of all of the roommate pairs that invite evening visits. Both men and women mention the simple evening sensations of clean sheets and pajamas, dim lighting, and quiet hallways that contribute to the pleasure of evening television. Some share special food or drinks at this time of day, and they recount the related activities and conditions under which they can most fully relax and enjoy themselves.

Roommates seem to take more pleasure in the experience when it is shared. But constraints against the option to share routines remain extremely high. Yet, three distinct roommate styles are observed among the tenured roommates at Hilltop. Each style is identified according to the degree of coordination that roommate pairs are able to achieve.

The first pair discussed here are Clark and Charlie, who exhibit a higher than average level of coordination. They readily agree that they experience a great deal of satisfaction from their television routine in the evenings. They watch together nearly every night, both tending to be in their room by 8:00 in the evening. With the door to their semiprivate room closed for the night, they take turns in the shared bathroom preparing for bed while the other "warms up the set." They usually watch late into the night with one or the other dozing off before the set is finally turned off for the night, usually sometime after the 11:00 news. They manage what has to be considered a successful roommate relationship according to their own terms, through coordinating their television viewing, and watching the same television at the same time.

Coordination with roommates is one important indicator of the pleasure derived from television consumption in the evening hours, and it also influences the amount of television used overall. But not all roommate pairs share the degree of coordination that Clark and Charlie do. For others, this pattern would not be ideal, even if it is achievable. Other pairs exhibit one of two other viewing patterns, with the three distinct styles serving as both cause and consequence of different experiences of the medium and each other.

Visits with roommate pairs in their semiprivate rooms also reveal the physical manifestations of the dynamics of their relationships. Furniture arrangements are a highly visible marker of coordination, or the lack of it. Those who coordinate television use tend also to co-orient their furniture to accommodate a television between them (see Figure 6.1). Clark and Charlie typify this arrangement with beds arranged side by side and a television set opposite, between the

FIGURE 6.1. Co-Oriented Roommate Style

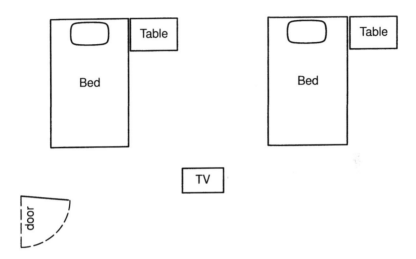

foot end of their beds. More common are those who have either developed a parallel style, or the more independent style that typifies transient roommate relations.

In the parallel style, both use their own television sets and adopt a more private, individual consumption stance, perhaps coordinating some of their other domestic routines, but tending to view television alone (see Figure 6.2). The more difficult transient situations engender a highly private consumption stance, some without any observable coordination.

Eileen and her roommate Alice, who both indicate a positive relationship with each other and also express a high level of satisfaction with their time use in the evenings, typify the preference for a parallel style. Their furniture arrangement is quite different from Clark and Charlie's room, with the beds facing each other, one side mirroring the other half of the room. They like different television programs, and both like to be very close to the sets so they can keep the picture close and the volume low. Their televisions sit on tables next to the head of their beds. The relationship relies on each roommate being sensitive to the other's situation. Eileen explains the difficulties of this style:

TELEVISION IN THE NURSING HOME

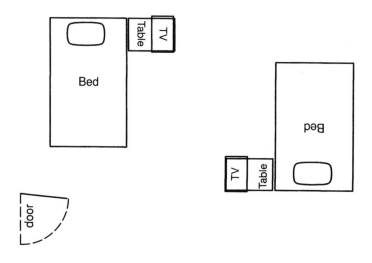

FIGURE 6.2. Parallel Roommate Style

> I don't want to interfere with her when she's watching a program so I'll pull my curtain and I'll watch mine, but we have to put them down low, but then I can't hear and understand talking going on when there's other noise in the background.

Once Alice has fallen asleep, however, Eileen feels more comfortable watching her television. She often makes plans to be out of the room in the early evening. If she stays in, she says, she keeps busy with another activity like reading that doesn't interfere with Alice as she tries to fall asleep.

Bert, however, has seen several roommates come and go recently. After the death of his last roommate he hoped to be paired with someone who was already living at Hilltop, but the other bed, which happens to be the closest to the nurses' station, was assigned to a "hospital transfer" instead. He lobbies periodically to be moved a couple of rooms down, and wishes for greater stability in his roommate situation. But Bert expresses doubt that he and his current assignment will ever become friends. He expects that this roommate will not survive for long and so he says he is unwilling to get to know anything about him just yet. Harsh in his judgment of the other man's vocal expressions of pain, when Bert spends any time in his room, he pulls the curtain separating himself from the critically ill man in the next bed so he can completely avoid all contact.

Although the three examples given here are reflective of three distinct roommate styles, it should be noted that while coordination appears to be desirable, neither the parallel nor co-oriented style should be considered preferable over the other. Each seems to emerge from the individual needs of the roommates, the desire and ability to adapt to each other, and the tenure and depth of the particular relationship. More important is the degree of satisfaction each feels, and the perception of roommate compatibility.

It should also be noted that consumption style is not always as rigidly enacted as the preceding examples illustrate. Roommate pairs combine styles to reflect desire for occasional co-orientation along with the exercise of individual interests. Even those who share most of the time, like Clark and Charlie, still have their own television sets and they keep the option to watch something alone, even if their tendency is to coordinate.

Furthermore, roommate situations tend not to remain stable for long periods of time, and residents are realistic about the length of time they can expect to stay together. Those who have been in the facility for an extended stay of a year or more have all had more than one roommate. The most transience seems to occur within the first half of the first year. The residents who are not expected to stay long experience higher roommate turnover since they are paired with others who are also considered short term. Since there are fewer men than women in the facility, incompatibility may be somewhat more likely for men. Bert's situation, then, while not uncommon, is one that Hilltop administration tries to avoid.

The degree of compatibility that Charlie and Clark share is somewhat unusual, but it is attributable to the degree to which they both desire, and are able to coordinate daily routines. Charlie and Clark expect a night nurse will check in on them at a predictable time after the late news, but they also know it will be a nonintrusive good night. They keep the television on until after she comes in, as a routine marking the time of day and the expectation of her arrival.

The television seems to signify alertness for them, even if both doze off before the nurse arrives, and she is the one who turns off the set.

Compatibility is clearly desirable in roommate pairings, but from an administrative point of view, social compatibility is not as essential as the compatibility of medical needs. However, medical compatibility is not completely unrelated to social compatibility. Although Clark and Charlie can more fully relax because they anticipate not being disturbed in the night, those who are subject to night intrusion may be more comfortable paired with someone else who has similar needs.

Taken together, the three roommate pairs illustrate the degree to which social coordination defines several aspects of the television viewing experience. When the distinction between coordinated and noncoordinated modes of media consumption in the domestic relationship is considered, it crudely predicts the amount of television consumed, the pleasure derived from the experience, and whether other needs (e.g., the need for intellectual stimulation) are going to be gratified.

One yield of such performance-centered study is documentation of the formal structure, or a logic of everyday media routines. Using the notion of a "trajectory," de Certeau (1984) speaks to the temporal and spatial aspects of media routines that are organized through adherence to the consumer's own particular logic. This approach allows the plotting of activities over large units of time and space, focusing on the "lived logic" of participants as an organizing principle. It is the elaboration of this logic that is the goal of social action research, compatible with the conceptual scheme employed by Anderson and Meyer (1988) in ethnograpic study of media audiences. Ethnographies identify individual premises of action, and coordination results from communal themes of action.

Derived from accounts of behavior, premises of action show how coordinated activity is accomplished with others. From this perspective, effects of the mass media are most readily observed in discourse through themes that emerge. Coordination is also evident in shared beliefs, stories, metaphors, and myths. The links between individuals are forged from particular, individual performances to the recognizable routine for which they account, through the premise of action that guides such a performance.

Radway's (1984) study of a community of romance readers illustrates the type of explanatory link sought here between performance, typification scheme, and communal theme of action. Using ethnographic description, Radway shows how the consumption practices of romance readers reflect the demands of daily life and are typified by readers as a constructive use of time. In their reasoning she finds links to the communal themes of "self-improvement" and "restorative self-nurturing," themes which Radway argues are reflected in the criteria readers use to evaluate potential reading material.

Through the comparison of premises of action, it is possible to demonstrate sources of congruence where individuals such as Clark and Charlie share premises of action, and sources of discord where premises of action are in conflict within a particular community. To this end, personal accounts are the best record of details that reflect personal definitions of experiences.

What follows in the next chapter is an accounting of how, when asked, nursing home residents justify and account for their media consumption activities. Probing these informants about significant events in their lives, their consumption routines, and the everyday practices they maintain in the nursing home, yields a variety of organizing principles that exert influence on everyday behavior. A more detailed portrait of eight key informants is illustrated with brief discussions of the organizing premises that emerge from the accounts of their behavior.

Chapter 7

Key Informants

Beyond the first set of interviews guided by protocol, eight individuals serve as experts, informing on aspects of their everyday life at Hilltop. Each of the eight profiled here was able to participate in lengthy recorded conversations aimed at elaborating the intricacies of their communication environment. Their quotes accompany descriptions of some everyday routines. However, some introductory comment is necessary to avoid leaving the impression that the experiences of this group are representative of the nursing home experience as a whole.

First, these residents have all managed successful adjustment to the nursing home. They are included as informants precisely because they have achieved tenure, as tenure is the single most important qualification to a long-term research strategy. The mean tenure of this group is extremely high, at more than four years, compared to the average stay of 2.6 years.

Even if what it means to succeed in the nursing home will be highly individualized, the degree of competence exhibited in negotiating nursing home routines is another indicator of this group's success, as is knowledge of situationally appropriate rules, and the ability to respond strategically to institutional demands. These notions of success serve as an ideal, perhaps, but they also contain a caveat to generalization from their experience. The group is clearly "skewed" more healthy and emotionally stable than the nursing home population as a whole.

It warrants mention that the transience of the nursing home population does not permit other voices to surface here. The short-term convalescent, the rapid-decline terminal patient, and the severely demented all exert a significant presence in the facility. Yet, the logistics of this project do not permit maximum representation of these residents. But because their influence does provide such a strong presence with broad implications for study of this social world, care is taken to represent them as fully as possible within the accounts of the informants who are more able to share their experience.

Second, the ages of this group range from thirty-nine (Gerry) to ninety years (Clark), with a mean age of seventy-five years. However, when the thirty-nine-year-old informant is factored out, the mean age rises to about eighty years, which is typical of the resident profile. While most nursing home residents are over seventy years, Gerry serves as a reminder that it is circumstance and not age that determines the need for assisted living, and her experience allows some speculation about future needs of care facilities when others of her cohort enter long-term care. In addition, three of the eight informants are married, two are divorced, and three are widowed. The three married residents are all under the mean age of eighty years, while those widowed are all over eighty years.

All of the residents in this informant pool are white, which reflects the local demography. Although three black women did enter the facility during the course of the study, none stayed long enough to participate. Because there are only a few nonwhite local residents, the likelihood of their achieving tenure in the facility remains statistically small.

These eight acknowledge that they have made a successful transition into long-term care. They express satisfaction with daily life in the facility, although their dissatisfaction is also clear. In more than a few cases, they report that their views depart significantly from prior beliefs and expectations they held of nursing home life. From anticipating death or complete disability, they now appreciate some aspects of daily life in the nursing home. Their stories express more fully what life is like in long-term care.

Estelle

After working for thirty-four years in the kitchen of a university dormitory, Estelle retired at the time of her husband's death, over twenty years ago. She is now eighty-six years old, with one relative she describes as "very close," a niece, Cindy, who is "like a daughter" to her. Cindy takes her shopping and sees to her bills and other business affairs. Although Estelle has a daughter of her own, she has not seen her in a decade. However, she visits with her niece often, usually at the nursing home. She also goes to Cindy's house for family holiday celebrations. With the doctor's permission, Estelle can stay overnight once in a while if she wishes.

Cindy is her sister's daughter. Before moving to the nursing home, Estelle tried living with her sister and her husband. Having fallen down the stairs a few times in her own home, the doctor advised her not to live alone. But the sister's living arrangement ended in bitter financial disagreement that has not yet been resolved. Estelle now has lived in the nursing home for two years, and she says she is happy there. Preferring not to impose on family members, she says the nursing home gives her the independence she wants and she especially enjoys the freedom she now has from domestic chores.

If she feels the urge to cook something she can use the activity room kitchen facility. But, she says, she is relieved that no one is dependent on her labor at this time in her life. She likes the availability of services the nursing home offers—the laundry, housekeeping, and particularly the beauty shop. Taking pride in her appearance, she frequently consults her mirror to adjust her white curls. She accessorizes the few outfits she owns with a small collection of costume jewelry.

Estelle views her side of the room as an extension of herself, taking the same care of her possessions as she does of her personal appearance. Having shared a room with a succession of women, she counts two that have moved on among her best friends, and she stays in touch with them mostly by telephone. But her current roommate, whom she does not yet know well, is a new arrival who spends much of her time in medicated sleep. Their two beds are arranged side by side with a night stand between them, a furniture arrangement that is Estelle's choice. But Estelle prefers to keep the privacy curtain between the beds pulled halfway most of the time.

Estelle's side of the room is distinctly recognizable from the barren other side. She has small objects fashioned from paper and yarn taped to the walls. Other memorabilia rest on every available surface. Estelle says she likes to entertain guests in her room whenever she has the opportunity. She offers a sweet or a drink from her small refrigerator as a show of hospitality, and she explains any new additions to the collection of mementos she has adorning her room. Estelle's television, like the other objects in her room, is a source of pride for her with a story of its own. She proudly relates that it is the only television she has ever owned. Her niece helped her acquire the set only recently after a stay in the hospital where, influenced by a roommate, she became "addicted" to daytime soap operas.

To decide how she will spend her time, Estelle keeps the monthly activity calendar handy, consulting it frequently. Of all the activities, she likes getting dressed up to go to the facility's church services best of all. She attends every weekly church-related function, including the Sunday afternoon services with a visiting minister, Bible study, and ladies' circle. She also attends most of the musical entertainments, looking forward to hymn sings especially and any visiting musician who comes to the facility. She is fond of the weekly bingo game as well, listing the game among the other church-related functions she attends. She also enjoys engaging in craft projects such as the ten Christmas baskets she recently decorated for family and friends.

Although she likes to get out of her room for meals and perhaps one social activity each day, the rest of the time Estelle spends in her room. When she is in her room and awake, she has the television on. Accompanied by the constant presence of the television set, Estelle is always busy with some activity. She describes television as "a partner" to the many projects in which she engages.

Estelle's account is used to illustrate two premises that organize her everyday routines: friendships are essential, and it is important to stay busy. She integrates both ideas into her daily routines by expending most of her effort engaged in craft activities that result in gifts for her friends. Estelle justifies her media consumption, then, as an accompaniment to work activities. The work activities that consume much of her time employ most of her temporal resources even when she is alone. Estelle spends her time creating the gifts she exchanges with her family and friends, and caring for her own possessions, many of them gifts she has received from others. Whenever she has the opportunity for conversation, she spends time talking to others about her work and about the people important to her.

These activities also include the television as a structural presence that she integrates into her work routines. Estelle's television choices follow, being high-frequency media choices like soap operas that mesh with her work routines. High-frequency media activities tend to be short events that occur frequently. The rhythm of Estelle's day is punctuated by few activities that occur outside of the room. She chooses these carefully, preferring religious and musical events that she considers worthy of the effort it takes to attend.

Estelle's television is, perhaps, her most prized possession. She finds many opportunities to recount the story of its origin as a gift from her niece. Also from the description of Estelle's afternoon cleaning routine recounted earlier, it is evident that Estelle's television has an importance as a physical object that is inseparable from the other objects in her room, including her refrigerator and her mementos. She cares for her television as she does all of her possessions, dusting and rearranging them daily, and taking pride in her ownership.

She also takes a great deal of pride in her craft activities, spending time each day working on projects that will ultimately be given as gifts. Because Estelle's television use usually accompanies the other activities that she engages in, her television routines might be construed as playing a structural role in organizing her activities. However, more valid is the reverse explanation that her activities punctuate her media consumption. Regardless of which activity dominates the interaction, the structuration primarily serves an expressive end in carving out a time and space for creative activity. This routine is compatible with the general sense of order that Estelle assumes in all of her media activities. She routinely reads a section of the newspaper, for example, at a particular time of day. This establishes a structured expectation for each day part. Just as the end of a television program prompts her to go to dinner, media routines serve as other markers as well, cuing activities and responses. As they lend structure to her day, they serve as markers to other people too, demonstrating her competence and control over her surroundings, and telling others that she engages in important activities that occupy her time.

Eileen

Widowed for a second time in 1980, Eileen has spent fifty-eight of her ninety years in marriage. She was the only girl in her family, and the last of her five brothers died in 1980, the same year as her husband. Eileen retired, sold her home and her retail clothing business in 1984, and moved into an apartment to be closer to her only son. However, after a series of strokes five years ago left her temporarily unable to walk or use her hands, at age eighty-five she moved into the nursing home.

Coming from a large family, Eileen has nieces and nephews all over the country that she stays in touch with, but her son Bill is the one on whom she depends. He visits her often, calls her almost every day, and takes care of all of her business affairs, providing her with any material needs not available within the facility.

With thick, dark hair, square shoulders, and a strong, deep voice, Eileen most often dresses in brightly-colored sweat suits that contribute to a more youthful look that belies her ninety years. Although she uses a wheelchair, she most often uses it as a walker, pushing it where she wants to go. She is active and attends many of the nursing home functions and likes the company and diversion they offer. When she leaves her room for a meal or a planned activity, she typically makes several social calls along the way that keep her away from her room for two hours or more. In this way, she makes the most of her energy visiting with friends, chatting with others in the hallway, and perhaps making a stop at the activity room before returning to her own room again. By making frequent stops she controls her exertion and marks a circuitous route that varies each time, returning at regular intervals to her room.

Eileen enjoys spending time in her room too, and she has taken time to make it a comfortable place. Her side of the room is crowded with several matching pieces of antique furniture—a small table, a chest of drawers and a bedside table. These, two lamps, and the oriental carpet on the floor are the only pieces she saved when she sold the rest of her household furnishings several years ago when planning her move into Hilltop. The furniture sets the room apart from some of the others in the facility, giving the room an elegant, homelike appearance that contrasts sharply with the hospital atmosphere in some of the other rooms.

Eileen, too, feels good about her decision to move to the nursing home and says she is living in the nursing home by choice. She came there to be independent, not wanting to lean too heavily on her son and his wife. Besides, if she lived with them, she says, she would spend her days alone while they worked. She prefers a life with more activity. Eileen has been busy all of her life, running a business and taking care of a home which left her little time for entertainment pursuits, so she enjoys indulging some of them now. She recalls rarely having time to finish reading an entire book before her retirement, preferring instead to read short stories and magazine articles that could be completed in one sitting. Now she has the time but says she cannot concentrate to read for long periods without falling asleep. She does, however, read the newspaper thoroughly every day. But she says she only occasionally looks at the advertisements for pleasure because she no longer shops.

While she says she does not miss the shopping, there are other things she no longer can do that she does regret. Her hands do not work well enough to grasp a needle or a pen, so she says she can no longer do the embroidery that she loves or write a letter to a friend. Convinced that ceramic painting would be a good rehabilitative exercise to regain the use of her hands, she did quite a bit of the craft when she first entered the nursing home. However, after five years of not seeing any progress with her hands, she has gotten tired of ceramics and does not participate in it anymore. She says she has "stepped back" to leave it for those who cannot do anything else.

Careful not to disturb Alice, who might be resting, Eileen turns on the television at various times throughout the day, primarily for news. She pulls the curtain that separates the two halves of the room and keeps the volume low. Small considerations such as this are important to her. Eileen says overall she and Alice get along well, rating them as intellectually compatible too. "She's like me. We've got minds of our own. We think." Alice also reads the newspaper every day, and while they do not usually watch television together, they do talk about items of interest in the news.

Eileen's story illustrates several themes that indicate the premises of her actions. Independence is important to her, but she also values the social interaction that the facility affords. Like Estelle, Eileen has a primary relational tie outside of the facility, with her son and his wife. And although family is important to her, she has no desire to live with them. Independence and social activity are two themes that frequently arise in her interviews, pervading her conversations.

She prides herself in staying in touch with the world through the news media and using the information she gleans as a resource in conversations with others.

Through demonstrating her ability to do for herself, she also has earned a measure of status among the staff and residents. Eileen is a favorite among the staff because they see her as an example of a well-adjusted resident who gives them little trouble. Consequently she was one of the first to be introduced at the beginning of the field work. She remained a valuable early contact, introducing her network of friends and endorsing their participation.

Because she has established a number of social relationships within the facility, she is able to spend much of her day engaged in conversation with people. Her friends include both residents and staff. Currently she is probably closest to her roommate, Alice, but a number of other people at Hilltop have known her longer than Alice.

Eileen is now somewhat limited in her ability to "do for herself" in some ways. Missing the manual dexterity that allowed her to write letters, dial the telephone, and change television channels readily, she continues to have other expressive outlets. Eileen is mobile enough to still enjoy a comparatively active social life. She takes pleasure in mealtimes and other scheduled activities for the opportunities they provide to interact. Perhaps the greatest pleasure she derives from her roommate is in the conversations they share on a wide range of topics.

For Eileen, then, media almost exclusively seem to serve a pre-communicative function. Enhancing her self-worth, she gains status with others through her social activity. Eileen makes the most of her few resources, principally her mobility and the knowledge she gathers from her news consumption. These allow her to spend much of her day engaged in conversation.

Margaret

Married for fifty-seven years, Margaret is now seventy-eight years old. She is a small woman, thin, and not quite five feet tall. She has bright blue eyes and an impish face that crinkles in a hundred places when she smiles. She smiles often, particularly when she is talking about her family. Her husband maintains the family home across town and visits her nearly every day. She also has three daughters and a son. While the girls are all married and raising families in other states, her son still lives locally, so she is able to see him and his two children fairly often. Separated geographically from the rest of her family, she has only seen pictures of her four great-grandchildren, but she stays in touch with them and her other nine grandchildren by telephone and frequent letters.

Both Margaret and her husband have been retired from the construction business since 1977. She worked as a secretary, and he worked as a builder for the same local company for over twenty years. Since retirement, she says, they have spent most of their time together, reading, watching television, playing cards with friends, and enjoying their garden. Now that Margaret has been in the nursing home for more than a year, she spends most of her day reading and watching television. She builds her day around the visits with her husband. She says she especially misses her friends and her home, and she has only a few visitors outside of her immediate family.

Margaret is being treated for a leg injury and for rheumatoid arthritis which severely limits her mobility, especially of her hands. She does not socialize with the residents of the nursing home outside of her room. She feels that her stay, however long, is still temporary, and that her primary social ties are with family and friends on the outside. Consequently, she takes all of her meals in her room, which has few personal touches and looks more like a hospital room than residential space. She is one of the few long-term residents without even a reading lamp, depending on the overhead fluorescent fixtures for all of her lighting needs.

Hopeful that she can soon return home, she also fears it because it would overburden her husband. Besides, "There are some things a woman does better," she says of the assistance she gets with personal hygiene from the nursing home staff.

Margaret starts her day with television news and weather, a new routine she established in the nursing home. She used to sleep later at home, but she cannot now because of the early morning noise. She fills her afternoons with soap operas while waiting for her husband to call. In the evenings after her husband leaves, she watches the television until she is ready to sleep. When she is not watching television, she is likely to be reading. She subscribes to six magazines and says she reads two or three romance novels each day, all of which are delivered by her husband when he visits. He picks up paperback novels for her at a secondhand book shop in town and brings them with her mail and the newspaper after he has finished it at home.

Margaret's experience of the nursing home is quite different from Estelle and Eileen's. The differences are reflected in the premises that organize her activities. Margaret's actions are guided by the premise that her stay in the nursing home is temporary, since her home is with her husband outside of the facility. He functions as the major resource in her life. He continues to be her primary social relationship; through him, Margaret is able to maintain other ties with the world outside of the facility. Because he visits daily, she says she feels no need to socialize outside of her room. Therefore, the relationships with her roommate and the staff who provide her care are the only ones she has encouraged during her stay.

Margaret may live for several more years in the facility. Her medical status is not likely to improve, and her husband is unable to care for her daily needs at home; thus a return to her former life is not imminent. For her, however, the nursing home is a convalescent facility only, and her belief in its transience is upheld by her activities and reflected in the impersonal appearance of her room. Even her reading materials are quickly whisked away into a shopping bag as soon as she finishes them, leaving no clue as to how long she has been there, how long she will stay, or how she spends her time. In fact, the television is the only visible personal effect in the room. Its presence highlights the sterility of the rest of the environment.

Given the prominence of the television in the room, it is no wonder she spends so much time with it on. It is also not unusual that some of its uses have little to do with the programs she chooses. Margaret uses the television as a communicative extension of herself. She uses it to signify awakeness, a willingness to interact, and the need for privacy. Because it is almost always on, it seems to be little more than moving images that serve as a convenient background. However, it also provides an important entry for Margaret and her roommate, Lillian, to engage in conversation. Even when reading or otherwise engaged, they both monitor the television as well.

Only leaving the area for physical therapy, bathing, or other care procedures, the two women spend the rest of their time within the small space of their room. Limited mobility increases the importance of the television for communicative purposes. It is not only a source of information about the world outside, but a form of stimulation. The television is employed strategically to define the conversational space, both including and excluding interactants. The television serves the function, for Margaret, of managing intimacy in a confined area. Obtaining a measure of privacy to visit with her husband is achieved by pulling the privacy curtain between the beds and strategically employing the television to create a separate space. Closing off the rest of the facility, her use of the television provides the opportunity to be alone with him while in the midst of noise and activity.

Bert

At sixty-seven years of age, Bert has been in the nursing home for five years, recovering from a stroke that affected the left side of his body, leaving him unable to walk, talk, or use his left hand. After a long, slow recovery, most of his motor functions have returned. Although he could live independently again if he wanted to, he says he is all right where he is, not having anyone in particular he would like to live with. Divorced after thirteen years of marriage, Bert has four children who live in the same state, but he is out of touch with two of them. He claims not to know how many grandchildren he has.

His thinning hair is neatly parted and combed back from a round face that breaks frequently into a jack-o-lantern grin, exposing the few yellowed teeth he has left. He draws deeply on a cigarette as he talks, but neglects to dispose of the ash, so he constantly has to brush the residue from his red sweatpants. An engaging social presence, he makes friends easily by offering bubble gum from the pocket in his blue cardigan sweater that was a gift from the daughter he now sees once or twice each year.

Bert says he is supported by the veterans benefits he earned in the Army when he served in Hawaii during World War II, a time he looks back upon fondly. However, his money does not go very far. Having just a few dollars left after his expenses are paid, he spends the remainder on cigarettes. An older sister, Betty, herself recently widowed, has lately begun to visit him more frequently. Bert also has a twin sister, Bertha, who is his closest relative. She lives with her husband just outside of town. Bertha visits him regularly, gives him pocket money when she can spare it, and brings him candy and baked goods to satisfy his sweet tooth. Bertha also gave him a gift subscription to *TV Guide* for Christmas after he told her that he had cancelled his delivery of the local paper because it was getting too expensive. He says that the only thing he really missed from the newspaper was the TV listings.

Mainly, he says, he just spends his time sitting around and thinking too much. He fights depression with humor, however, joking with his friends, and teasing the young women on the staff. Watching television mostly, he never has been much of a reader, and he scrupulously avoids almost all of the facility's organized activities. His daily routine has not changed much since he entered the facility, he says, although everything now takes him longer than it used to. He still rises before dawn and goes to bed by eight o'clock in the evening. This is a routine he established during his years of farming when he also established a pattern of heavy television use in the winter when there were fewer outdoor responsibilities. On television he likes to watch sporting events and movies. Old westerns are his favorites. Not liking to be reminded that he cannot dance anymore, he says he does not listen to music very often, but he turns on the radio at night sometimes when he has trouble sleeping. Mostly, he says, he use radio and television to block out the sounds of other people's discomfort that frequently disturb his sleep at night.

Bert divides his time between the table in the smoking lounge and his room across the hall, going back and forth throughout the day. When he is sitting in the smoking lounge, others are likely to gather to talk, smoke, and watch weather and segments of old movies on cable television. Enjoying the company of other men, he and his friends are sharply critical of the residents who exhibit any signs of dementia. They resent the dual use of the smoking lounge as a place for the staff to deposit incommunicative residents in front of the television. Rolling his eyes when he talks about these residents, Bert attributes their problems to "giving up on life." He leaves the lounge when he feels he and his friends are outnumbered, and they no longer have control over the television.

Bert's activities illustrate several organizing premises. Because mobility ranks high among the faculties that Bert values, he attributes his present level of physical activity to the effort he expended in regaining his strength during his stroke recovery. Furthermore, he credits his level of mobility for a high level of social interaction in which he engages. He also credits his mobility for the degree of selectivity he is able to exercise in media consumption.

Bert operates under the premise that the appearance of competence is foremost and that he alone is fulfilling his own needs. Family ties are not at the center of Bert's social life, nor does he have a strong roommate bond as Eileen and others have, but he maintains important friendships, particularly among the other male residents. Although he avoids most organized events, he selectively attends the few activities designed for the men, such as the card games and television sports, otherwise spending most of his time in the public smoking lounge where other men will stop by to visit.

He credits mobility, too, for his comparatively wide range of selection in media choices, where he exercises options not available to many other residents. He knows, for example, what movies are going to be shown on the cable channels he prefers. He attaches value to this knowledge, remarking often, "If you're going to watch television, you should know what's on." His unusually early morning routine is possible because he can move freely between his room and the lounge area, enabling him to watch his favorite movies at his convenience and with few interruptions. It is pleasurable for him, he says, because he has planned in advance what he will watch.

This freedom also brings him in contact with both the night crew and the morning staff in the quiet hours when most of the residents are still in bed. The ability to talk with the staff has allowed Bert to develop a relationship with some of the nursing staff that is more like friendship than caregiving. This has brought him privileges not enjoyed by many others. Bert is one of the few that is sometimes invited into the staff lounge, which is normally off-limits to residents. The staff lounge has the only microwave oven in the facility, which Bert uses sometimes to make soup or oatmeal.

Among Bert and his friends, exercising selectivity in making media choices is an important skill. In Bert's terms, this skill distinguishes "us" from "them." He means that those who are not critical of television choices are clearly not in control of their mental faculties. Bert exhibits competence, then, through critical use of the television, frequently changing the television channels. Bert expresses loud disapproval when he finds the smoking lounge television set tuned to cartoons, exiting the area only when he loses control of the set.

Adelle

Adelle is one of "them." At least that is what some of the residents say about her, because she is increasingly disoriented. Most of the time she lives in a past world that denies all of her present reality. She is widowed but usually does not remember the death of her husband. She speaks of him constantly, always in the present tense. She will also speak at length about her children as though they are young and still need her care. But they are adults now, and have been on their own for a long time. When her adult children visit, she treats them like neighbors who have come to call. She is friendly and pleasant, but does not recognize them as her children.

Adelle is aggressively friendly, entering into conversation with anyone who will stop and talk. She propels her wheelchair with pink-slippered feet, maneuvering to get close enough to hear those who speak with her, and she listens intently. With naturally dark eyelids and red cheeks, she gives the impression that she is wearing makeup, but a closer look that takes in her untamed hair and misbuttoned sweater corrects the impression. Carrying a large, nearly empty purse that she hunts through often, she never seems to find what she is looking for.

Accustomed now to being asked questions that she cannot answer, she still has enough cognitive capacity to socialize and to be embarrassed at her deficits. With tranquilizers to cut down on agitation, she is frequently disoriented, but works hard attempting to cover it up. She has learned to use one of several verbal strategies to deflect the questions or disguise her memory loss. Sometimes she will say she has to sit down and figure out the answer, if she can respond tomorrow. Or, she will say, "I'll ask my husband when he comes home." Other times she is just vague. Instead of giving a date, she will say "It's been a long time," or for a place she answers "Just south of here." When pressed she sometimes gets angry and says "It's like I just told you," refusing to elaborate further.

Although she becomes momentarily agitated when confronted with her losses, in general she is pleasant and sociable. When the activity staff members come to get her to participate in some event, she always cheerfully goes along. Perhaps some of her mood is attributable to the tranquilizers prescribed for her, but much can be credited to the vestiges of her fading personality. She has always been friendly and outgoing. Other residents remember when she first entered the facility and was more lucid. Then she often entertained the dining room with one of her songs and told stories that made everyone laugh.

Although she has lost many of her faculties, Adelle maintains a strong adherence to a work ethic that proscribes idle time. When asked about her television consumption, which is how she spends most of her day now, she will deny that she has any time at all for such a frivolous pursuit. She says she has too much housework to do and that raising a family properly requires all of her spare time. She says, too, that she has no interest in following the news and that she hears everything she needs to hear about the world from her next-door neighbor.

Adelle's denial of her level of television consumption illustrates one of the premises that organize her activity, although her behavior violates that premise, which creates a major source of conflict for her. As Bert's notion of selectivity marks for him a distinction between competence and incompetence, so Adelle's recognition of the same premise is evident in her denial.

Although she holds the desire to appear in control, she has largely lost the means to do so. In reality, she spends most of her time each day watching the television screen in her room or in the lounge when someone on staff wheels her there. Her television viewing has become entirely nonselective, however. She never changes the channel and cannot follow a simple plot, although she does express enjoyment when she watches the screen. While she states her disapproval of television use when questioned about it, her behavior while in front of the television suggests that she takes pleasure in the activity. Smiling and relaxing in her demeanor, she appears to take greater pleasure from the television than she does from her interactions with people. Perhaps this is because the conversational demand is low, and little response is required of her by the television set, which does not judge her deficits.

Clark

Relocating frequently when he was a young man, Clark had a series of jobs after college, primarily in retail management. These jobs led him all over the Midwestern and Eastern United States. He enjoyed traveling and enjoyed being single, not marrying until he was forty-one years old, when he fell in love with a woman twenty years younger than he. He is now eighty-eight years old. He looks like a man accustomed to bachelorhood, with missing shirt buttons replaced in the wrong color, and a broken zipper held together with safety pins. He keeps his reading glasses, now taped together, in a case in his shirt pocket when he is not wearing them. Clark carries one of his portable radios on his wheelchair and holds it next to his ear, so he does not disturb others with the volume. Clark has two children and three grandchildren that visit him, but not often. Although his former wife is still alive, living and working locally, they have been separated a long time, and he hears very little about her now, only from his children.

Clark has been in the nursing home for six years, longer than anyone else who now lives there. He entered three months after it opened. Thus he speaks with authority about the changes in management and policy and the growth from sixty-four residents to his current estimate of 140. He entered the nursing home after an accident in which he broke his leg in three places. The accident left him permanently unable to walk.

Clark did not retire until his accident. Although unemployed, he says he is surprised at how little idle time he has now. He used to work ten or fifteen hours a day and he maintained an active, after-hours social life, rarely sleeping more than five hours in a night. Now he wonders how he did it all. He tires easily from simple daily tasks such as shaving and dressing, and most of his energy is expended in pushing his wheelchair from place to place.

Clark shares a room with Charlie, and the two of them consider each other good friends. They have slipped into an easy routine, and they have gotten closer since Charlie's wife died a few years ago. They both read a lot, sharing books and magazines. They both selectively attend some of the programs offered by the activity department although not usually together, except for the weekly men's card game. They also like similar television programs that they watch together on Charlie's set. Clark has six radios that are each assigned a different purpose. They include one to wake him up with, one to go to sleep, one for ballgames, and the portable for his wheelchair. But Charlie's hearing is poor, so Clark's radios never disturb him.

Clark's activities are organized by several important premises of action that guide his performance. First, Clark arranges his day with frequent activity changes, operating on the premise that being busy is the key to combating boredom, appearing vital, and feeling good about his day. Frequent activity changes give the impression that Clark is highly selective in his media choices. But he denies being very rigid in his tastes, saying that he is actually open to almost anything, allowing Charlie to dictate many of their television choices. Their television consumption is as much an opportunity to converse as it is to be entertained, he says. However, the solitary activities he engages in, such as his reading and radio consumption, serve as more personalized modes of expression.

He exercises far more selectivity in choosing reading materials and radio programming than he does with television. Clark articulates specific criteria for the kinds of things he is likely to enjoy by himself, such as mystery stories and articles about fishing, ballroom dance music, and jazz. Yet, he speaks emphatically about the role that media play in his social life and expresses a desire to share other people's interests. He is aware that he uses his media activities to create bonds between himself and others, especially with Charlie, his roommate.

Clark's story illustrates a roommate relationship that is a particularly strong tie for both of them. Unlike Margaret, who through her husband maintains a social life outside of the nursing home, neither of the men consider anyone outside the facility especially close to them anymore. Clark has established a moderately active pattern within the nursing home and he says he feels it is important to take advantage of some of the scheduled activities the facility offers. Otherwise he spends his time reading, listening to the radio, and watching television. Accustomed to a busy lifestyle, he gets tired of any one medium before long. His days are spent moving constantly from one media activity to another when he is not engaged in personal care routines or traveling the lengthy course back and forth to the dining room.

Dan and Gerry

Dan and Gerry met in the nursing home and married five years ago in a ceremony attended by a few family members, and residents and staff from the facility. For their honeymoon, Gerry was moved across the hall into Dan's room, where they arranged two hospital beds side by side and pooled their few possessions. They spent months negotiating with the staff to establish privacy routines that were acceptable to all. Now staff members observe a knock-and-wait policy before entering, a privilege not enjoyed by any other residents.

This is a third marriage for sixty-three-year-old Dan. Gerry, at thirty-nine, is twenty-five years younger than Dan, and this is the first time she has been married. Dan has dark hair, parted and slicked down, and tattoos on both arms that make it easy to envision him as a truck driver, a job from which he took an early retirement when rheumatoid arthritis began to severely impede his driving. He says he entered the home when sclerotic arteries caused a blood clot in his leg that required major surgery and ultimately took away his ability to walk.

Gerry is blond, pretty, and self-conscious about the weight she has gained since she's been ill. She worked in retail sales until 1983 when the store she worked for closed. She was diagnosed with multiple sclerosis at about the same time. Knowing she would never improve enough to care for herself, she entered the nursing home at age thirty-three when she began to lose muscle coordination and needed daily help.

Dan and Gerry adhere to a rigid, daily schedule, which they say they find comforting. They have the television on every free minute of the day, whenever they are not out of their room for lunch or dinner, sleeping, or occupied with care routines. Although Dan used to read quite a bit, particularly in the period after his second wife died, he says he reads very little now, preferring to spend his time with Gerry. He says that when he wants to he is capable of reading at the rate of two hundred pages an hour. At that speed he quickly read nearly every book in the local library, but he now finds reading less satisfying than doing something with his wife. Gerry used to read quite a bit as well, but problems with her vision prevent her from reading now. Television, she says, is something they can do together.

Their style of television viewing is typical of couples and close family members with vision and hearing losses in the nursing home. They help each other when one of them misses something, as they often do. Gerry's sight problem makes her dependent on Dan's eyes, and his hearing loss leads him to ask her to repeat dialog for him frequently. When they are engaged in a television program, they are usually in bed, which brings them physically close together. Even when the television is off they look for opportunities to be close, frequently holding hands. In conversation they often finish each other's sentences, and each has come to rely on the other's memory for details.

Dan and Gerry are an extremely close couple, but they have ways of expressing their individuality as well. They do spend time alone and separately with others, but they also share certain organizing premises essential to their creation of an identity as a couple. They operate under the premise that togetherness is preferable to solitary activity.

Creation of their couple status is the organizing premise behind their privacy routines, and influences shared media choices as well. This is particularly evident in the routines they have changed since their marriage. Taking pride in the ability to coordinate routines, they opt now to engage in much more television consumption together than either of them did separately. They also spend a substantial portion of their financial resources finding movies that they both will enjoy. They both mention tastes they used to indulge alone—she used to watch soap operas and romances, he used to like westerns and boxing matches—but now they spend most of their available time sharing television programs rather than pursuing their individual choices. Some of the changes can be looked at as attempts to minimize their individual losses, but it is also illustrative of strategic attempts to maximize their shared resources, evident in the examination of their coordinated activity.

Their story is also used here to highlight the difficulties that couples experience in trying to preserve a measure of intimacy in the nursing home environment. While there are not many couples living together in the nursing home, there are those such as Margaret who are married but unable to live together. Other couples are split into separate rooms, according to individual medical needs. And some are engaged in new relationships, having met in the facility. In addition to married and romantic pairs, there are also mother/daughter pairs and siblings residing in the nursing home who also desire time and space to be alone together.

Although Dan and Gerry are dependent on nursing care, they also consider the nurses' presence intrusive. Dan and Gerry have been quite successful in asserting their need for time and space to be alone, but others in the nursing home are less successful. To appreciate this accomplishment, it is important to place it in the context of the indignities that most couples endure. Dan and Gerry's struggles against the institutional rules demonstrate the difficulty that all residents encounter in relinquishing privacy in the public realm of an institutional environment. What is unusual about Dan and Gerry's situation is not the level of privacy that they desire. Most of the residents express the desire for more privacy than they have. What is unusual is the level of privacy that they have been able to achieve.

Dan and Gerry manage to create an intimate environment within the institutional setting by establishing routines that integrate high-frequency care demands with their other needs. Because shared time is important to them, they pool resources and strive for a common goal, engaging in activities that maximize their time together. Resources that Dan and Gerry employ include their money and time as well as their shared possessions and their individual abilities. For example, by taking advantage of Dan's mobility they are able to arrange nursing services on demand, something that Gerry was not able to achieve alone.

SUMMARY OF STAGE TWO

Stage Two of the research reports results yielded from the interview protocol, examining the media environment holistically and comparing residents' use of different media with their patterns of sociality. Media routines are shown to be the result of the ability to seek out preferences, enabled by more or less satisfying living conditions. The interview data support conclusions about some common program preferences in the nursing home and introduce the notion that roommate pairings influence the degree of pleasure derived from the television experience.

Some of the trends noted involve individual preferences for local media, certain game shows, and some forms of music television. But more evident than common trends in program preference, what emerges from the interviews is the variety in individual tastes and consumption styles.

Along with the preferences expressed for particular media and program types, the interviews illustrate the adaptation to environmental change, functional loss, and the institutional regimen. Overall, the levels of media use, and television especially, remain consistently high although varied in individual styles. While levels of depression and negativity also remain high, satisfaction with the environment and with media choices, and the pleasure derived from media use are still evident. Pleasure is enhanced by coordination, the ability to share media, and other everyday routines. Thus the quality of the roommate relation seems to be most indicative of the level of pleasure derived from the media experience.

Where television consumption is high, it does appear to operate as a substitute for other media, particularly where functional losses interfere with previous consumption routines. Yet, these substitutions appear not to encompass relationships as some theorists have suggested. Instead, roommate pairs who coordinate their media routines appear to consume more television and experience more pleasure in the activity. Consumption style emerges from the negotiation in roommate pairs and is related to the stability of the relationship between roommates. The ability to establish nontransient relations may be the key to a general sense of satisfaction and adjustment to the nursing home environment.

This section also establishes some premises of action that organize individual activity, and it links roommate pairs and other dyads through shared premises of action that illustrate their coordination. The television routines that Clark and Charlie establish to fill their evenings and the routines that Dan and Gerry observe when sharing a movie are both examples of coordinated activity. However, as Eileen's activity patterns indicate, not all coordination involves co-orientation, simultaneous consumption, or even a shared media selection. Coordination is an accomplishment of both shared activity and shared action premises. Coordination results from communication activities of compromise and negotiation, achievements that result in the ability to enact comforting routines.

The action premises illustrate organizing constructs in the lives of a group of informants who negotiate everyday life in the nursing home. As statements from long-term residents indicate, common themes include the importance of maintaining independence, staying active, expressing individuality, and creating privacy. Activity is shown to be motivated by the premises that guide individual action. These premises are related such that some tentative conclusions can be drawn about their impact on the media environment, downplaying the importance of any particular selection in favor of the logic that organizes activity.

Media consumption, too, has an important social dimension. The ability to employ some avenue of personal expression through media selection and other communicative means is important to the establishment of useful, structural routines as well as to the strategic creation of constructs such as privacy and competence. The next section builds an argument for closer examination of coordination in order to clarify the essential elements of coordinated interaction.

STAGE THREE: ANALYSIS AND CONCLUSIONS

Goals for the third and final stage are confirmation of results, and coherent presentation of the findings. Activities of this stage are further analysis of the interview data, clarification of the concepts explored, and conducting final interviews that confirm results. To that end, this section is organized according to the concepts' coordination, selectivity, and strategies.

One implication from the second stage of research is that high media consumption is not problematic if it is on some level selective. Television appears to enhance daily life in the nursing home and provide an attractive and accessible common resource. In Stage Three, these themes are developed further, addressing different modes of consumption and the mechanisms of selectivity. It also addresses the strategies that nursing home residents employ in response to their own needs and in relation to others. Additionally, the origins of those consumption strategies are discussed, suggesting that even newly established routines are rooted in past behavior, maintaining consistency with patterns established earlier in life.

Chapter 8

The Viewing Stance

Program preferences in long-term care should not be expected to be substantially different from tastes expressed by members of the same populations living outside of a nursing facility. As the survey responses indicate, content and genre preferences are diverse, with some partiality for local sources of news and other information, but otherwise spanning all genres and types of media. There is support for previous findings that establish that older people's tastes tend to lean toward serious content (Atkin, 1976) and realism (Kubey, 1980). However, it cannot be discounted that the primary motive for viewing serious material may still be entertainment. This might seem to be contradicted by confirmation of the prevalence of an escapist viewing pattern, a trend that is also evident in the literature (Mundorf and Brownell, 1990). But the conclusion that elder media use in long-term care is excessive and largely nonselective is not wholly warranted, an assumption that discounts the variety of functions that media serve, and the potential benefits of media use, even very heavy television use, in long-term care.

Viewing motive aside, it is clear that no single set of program preferences or viewing pattern should be anticipated, nor should any one style be considered most beneficial. However, examining the rationale by which content selections are made and the premises that motivate program selection provides insight into the functions media serve in long-term care, and can suggest interventions for those less capable of devising their own media consumption strategies.

Uses and gratifications research has tackled the issue of selectivity in attempting to transcend taste preference alone as a means of determining and explaining media effects. But research on the motives for viewing typically assesses consumption motives at only one time, usually long after the moment of consumption. Practical reasons alone prohibit collecting comparable data from those in long-term care, and among the oldest audiences in general, as memory may not be especially reliable. Motivations are likely to be confounded with gratifications obtained, and colored by rationalizations of the appropriate use of time. Because of the nature of field observation used in this study, a unique opportunity avails itself to compare residents' individual plans for consumption activities with observed use of time and retrospective accounts of media activities.

In most cases, there is poor fit between the three measures—anticipated media use, observed media use, and recalled consumption. In most cases residents' plans for media use are more in line with their recalled use, and at much lower levels than the amount of use observed. This is particularly true of the amount of television use compared with the use of other media, where the three measures tend to be more in agreement.

This finding suggests that there are at least two types of consumption strategies at work here, perhaps distinguishable by the categories familiar to media research of instrumental and ritualistic use, which have previously been used to distinguish selective and nonselective consumption. But instrumental use is not reducible to the fulfillment of a single need, such as the need to survey the outside world. And ritualistic use fulfills a variety of needs as well. Moreover in the nursing home, one might argue that ritualistic television viewing patterns could be the most instrumental strategies, filling time and providing stimulation among other functions, some of which are social.

The first of the measures, anticipated media use, refers to the consumption of any program or publication that is planned in advance. Some justifications that indicate anticipated media use and a planning of consumption activity do appeal to the habitual nature of routines:

> I know I'll read the newspaper tomorrow because I always do. Right after breakfast.

Other anticipated media events are singled out because they are special in some way.

> Oh, *Lion in Winter!* I love Katharine Hepburn. I'm not gonna miss that if I can help it.

Not all media events are anticipated. Residents of Hilltop, in fact, seem to "forget" activities with some regularity, particularly television consumption that is not planned in advance. Residents who participated in this study are regularly observed to be engrossed in a television program for an hour or more, yet they report later that they spent the afternoon engaged in some other activity. Although it is not possible to determine whether there is intentional deception in misreporting use of time, it is more likely there was nothing particularly memorable about the experience that would allow it to be understood as a primary activity. However, the notion that television constitutes a guilty pleasure that should be minimized cannot be discounted.

Margaret, for example, readily admits that she watches soap operas and reads romance novels. She does not express any concern that either is a particularly poor use of her time when she is interviewed. Yet, during a two-hour interview session with her roommate, Lillian, in their shared room, Margaret is observed oriented toward the television, enrapt in a soap opera, with a magazine spread open on her lap and its pages facing down. Afterward, she was asked about her activity.

W: I hope we didn't disturb you.

M: No, you was just fine.

W: What have you been up to today?

M: Just setting here reading the *Journal*.

W: Wasn't that *Guiding Light*?

M: Maybe, I wasn't paying much attention.

W: Daydreaming?

M: No, just reading.

She probably did finish the magazine, shifting her attention between magazine and television and perhaps elsewhere in the two-hour session. But why deny that the soap opera is the focus of her attention? The answer probably lies somewhere between the guilty pleasure that soap operas are assumed to be, and the fact that the soap opera in question is not one of Margaret's favorites.

It is not uncommon for television to be considered a secondary activity when it is mentioned at all in the activity surveys. Residents engage in a range of activities in front of the television, as in any domestic situation. However, if television is not seen as the primary activity, it is not necessarily verbally acknowledged. From the routines discussed earlier, it is clear that television maintains such a pervasive presence, and it serves such a variety of functions, that the term "watching" a particular program does not capture the nature of the activity, or the different activities implied.

Consider another example, when Estelle wants to talk about what she has been doing since the last interview session:

> E: Now see them baskets there? I fixed them. I fixed ten of them baskets. That one took me about two days and a half, that big one. And the little ones only took me a day and a half. I've got some back here, some under here.
>
> W: Very nice work. Did you do that while you were watching television?
>
> E: Yeah. I guess so. I can't remember.

Although Estelle responds that she cannot remember, she always has the television on in her room while she works. Thus the television accompaniment would be typical of her routine and would not require effort for recall. However, she says she cannot remember, probably because there is nothing exceptional about the programs she had on. Most important, it is clear she wanted admiration for her work and not a change in the focus of the conversation to ask about an activity that is only peripheral in her mind.

These examples illustrate the difficulty in assessment of media consumption practices using questions that rely on recall. But it also indicates that, for interview respondents, measurement of television use is confounded by critical appraisal of the quality and the quantity of television programs that are consumed. The difficulty of distinguishing between watching television and watching specific memorable programs is exacerbated by the poverty of language terms to distinguish the different interactions. But recall is enhanced in this study by providing the option that consumption might not have been a primary activity. After adopting an interview strategy of asking for activities that residents engage in that are accompanied by television or radio, recall of the amounts of individual consumption increase dramatically. Giving the option to report different modes of consumption, then, allows a better fit with the conception of how media are used.

When examining the coordinated activity of two or more interactants, the effect is even more pronounced. It involves multiple activities and compounds the equation with the complexity of the social interaction among them. Therefore, building a research vocabulary appropriate to discuss a logic of consumption practices involves establishing some basic units of analysis that respond to this set of group dynamics. In this case, modes of media consumption might profitably be considered to be constructed of a series of "stances," that are connected in space and time by a particular lived logic that the stances represent. That logic is contained in accounts of behavior that reveal the premises that guide individual behavior and indicate the degree of coordination with others. The stance is a behavioral manifestation of action premises, enacted with and in the presence of others.

Television is such an omnipresent entity in institutions and other domestic environments that allowance must be made for different modes of reception that accommodate other activities. For example, considering a process of engagement as roughly continuous, the lowest possible level of involvement would include instances of witnessing the media consumption of another, while generally ignoring the program or the content.

Witnessing the media consumption of others is quite common in the nursing home, as in any domestic unit. Take, for example, an interaction involving the two women, Bea and Barbara, mentioned earlier. Both women, friends who are in their late sixties, come together in the activity lounge nearly every morning. They get together for conversation, coffee and donuts, and whatever scheduled activity might be going on—perhaps ceramics or the weekly manicure sessions. Barbara, like most of the nursing home residents, uses a wheelchair. However, it does not seem to impede her level of social involvement since she attends most of the formally scheduled activities and makes use of the lounges and activity areas at other times. Like most of the other residents, Barbara has her own television set in her room. However, she prefers the company of others to the company of her noncommunicative roommate, so she faithfully watches her favorite game show and soap opera on the activity room television set each morning. Whatever activity she is engaged in ceases for Barbara after the game show contestants are introduced and the host announces the beginning of "round one."

Bea, on the other hand, is not fond of either of Barbara's program choices. While Barbara is occupied with her programs, Bea continues to engage in conversation or activities with others. More often Bea sits staring out of the large picture window located just to the left side of the television set. Bea likes Barbara's company. She remains in front of the television screen, although she has no interest in Barbara's television programs. Bea seems to be able to ignore the sound as well as the picture.

If Bea's stance, witnessing, is considered a low-level involvement, at the other end of the scale, the highest levels of involvement might be indicative of Barbara's stance, which is evident in her rapt attention and relative oblivion to the immediate surroundings. Communication research has largely been concerned with an ideal audience member, typified in Barbara's highly attentive stance, to the exclusion of other modes of reception. But coordination involves the linking of individuals in conjoined behavior. And individuals do not necessarily share the same program preferences, the same level of attentiveness, the same logical premises, or the same motivations for viewing.

The issue is not whether behavioral indicators such as orientation or eye contact adequately distinguish between high and low levels of cognitive engagement. Nor is it that such indicators are even a requirement for engagement. Instead the focus of this analysis is on the social factors involved that engender a less-than-ideal stance while still providing evidence of coordination.

Observation relies on behavioral cues, but as Anderson and Lorch (1983) note from their research with children, physical orientation and visual contact do not adequately account for nonvisual monitoring of television material. Monitoring more adequately describes Barbara's stance during the commercial breaks in her daytime television viewing. When she engages with Bea and others in the activity room in conversation, she still remains aware enough of the television to break conversation, sometimes in midsentence, when the program resumes. Monitoring might also be the stance adopted by Estelle as she engages in housekeeping and craft activities alone in her room, and even Margaret when she claims to be reading a magazine instead of watching the soap opera. However, the dynamics change with the addition of another person or persons in the consumption environment. Even the attentive consumption stance characterizing Barbara's style needs to be adapted to accommodate others in the consumption environment. Assessment here must transcend the traditional onset/offset behavioral accounting in favor of larger units that are more descriptive of the whole interaction.

The styles of consumption sometimes adopted by Clark and Charlie illustrate another consumption stance. In the afternoons, Charlie tends to doze or pick up a magazine while Clark is watching a television program. Charlie tends only to be drawn into the interaction by a cue from Clark that he is enjoying the show at this time of day. This consumption stance could be termed hitchhiking, a stance that involves a low level of awareness of media content, except to engage at cues from another person's affective responses. Laughter, for example, provides an affective cue that tends to draw others into a higher level of involvement in an attempt to share the pleasure. The difference between hitchhiking and monitoring is subtle, but important, because the cue to engage comes from another individual rather than as a response to a cue from the program.

It is important to reiterate that the issue of cognitive processing is not addressed at this level of analysis. Consumption, according to Peterson:

> shifts attention from how audiences understand or interpret media products to how habitual practices organize media audiences and texts. (1987, p. 38)

Borrowing a distinction made in the study of linguistics, ultimately, semantic production and the underlying cognitive processes depend not only on cognitive variables that tell us about consumption competence, but also upon the relational and situational constraints that influence consumption performance.

Whether reactive, preconscious, or more consciously controlled by the consumer, semantic production is both process and product of the interaction. According to Biocca (1988),

> ... the meaning of the television message, while constructed within the individual viewer and therefore by the viewer, may be largely constructed outside of consciousness, yet meaning may be the final product of a complex interaction of message form and content, contextual and situational factors, as well as the semiotic competence of the viewer, sociopsychological construction of the viewers' semantic associations and, finally, idiosyncratic processing dispositions. (p. 65)

The tendency for media research to focus on individual cognitive measures is indicative of a perspective that has tended to subordinate audience performance to competence, largely due to the prevalent study of children. Media research also attributes attentiveness in the receiver to individual difference variables, and to formal features of media content. While attention, concentration, and processing of media material occur largely within the individual, movement to a level of analysis where negotiation between individuals occurs allows discussion of concepts related to adult coordination such as locus of control.

There are a number of social factors in the nursing home, as in any domestic unit, that influence both attention and comprehension in performance rather than in potential. Because attention is enacted in coordination with others, the debate over sources of individual control may best be circumvented through an examination of the overall semantic product of the interaction as it unfolds. Attention is seen pragmatically as level of engagement, and processing of media material may be thwarted or enhanced through interaction in context. Thus, the process of moving from one level of engagement to another may occur frequently, or not at all, within a given temporal frame. Also, it will occur differently for members of the same group or household at any given time. Yet, it is possible to examine patterns of consumption as the tendency to engage/disengage over a period of time and to assess the meaning-product more holistically in relation to the context of interaction.

To illustrate this point, consider another incident from the nursing home. Although Bea and Barbara, as shown previously, have established a coordinated pattern of stances in relation to the daytime television programs, their interaction also responds to others in the environment. For example, one morning Helen, a small woman in her late seventies, wheeled herself into the activity room during Barbara's soap opera, an event that is not out of the ordinary. Helen is an avid reader, and she often comes to the activity room to peruse the magazines kept there while she visits with others. This particular morning, she parked her chair next to Bea at a large, round table located in view of the television. Helen sat casually turning the pages of a magazine and commenting on their contents, mostly to Bea, and Barbara sat nearby, engrossed in her soap opera. While so engaged, Helen overheard enough of the soap opera dialogue to determine that the topic explored in this scene was an abortion dilemma, and she expressed strong opinions as to the suitability of the topic for television.

Barbara's first response to Helen's commentary is to use the remote control to raise the volume, presumably to hear the program over the sound of the conversation. Bea, without knowing the details of the story line, continued the conversation, defending the morality of the soap opera in general. Barbara then lowers the volume until the program is inaudible, and then enters the conversation defending the way in which the topic has been handled.

This interaction shows that Barbara, who was initially reluctant to alter her stance, does so in order to defend the program's portrayal of a sensitive topic. Her initial response, raising the volume, may either be seen as an attempt to thwart the interruption, or possibly as an attempt to gather all the facts before entering the conversation. What is significant here is that the three women assume different consumption stances. Each uses the same program in a different way to express personal views. Furthermore, this interaction is not reducible to attention to the medium or comprehension of its meaning. The text of the program is appropriated differently by each woman and employed tactically as an opportunity for personal expression.

Some theoretical support for the idea of different modes of media consumption is drawn from de Certeau (1984), who argues that characteristics of the speech act can be found in many areas of everyday life. He advocates considering media consumption activity a form of enunciation.

Enunciation refers to the various activities, both cognitive and physical, that constitute media consumption. This conceptualization of the audience places the media consumer in the linguistic role of the "speaker." In a social context this perspective is particularly useful because observed modes of consumption are less attributable to individual abilities or to media content than to some dynamic of the environment.

Different modes of consumption are evident in examination of the coordinated behavior of participants in the media consumption environment. The consumption stance can vary among members of the audience for the same event. For example, a consumption stance may be associated with different program types for the same person. This would be reflected in one's tendency to watch news in a different mode than one would watch a soap opera. At other times, a stance may be more reflective of individual strategies since one might have a tendency to approach all consumption of a particular medium in the same way. If, for example, one looks at a magazine for fifteen minutes before going to sleep every night, the stance adopted by the reader could be seen as an individual strategy for inducing sleep.

Accounts of different modes of consumption allow the discussion of the strategic aspects of the concept labeled above as a stance. Consumption stances can be seen to form the basis on which larger media consumption patterns are constructed. The stances characterized here include witnessing, hitchhiking, and monitoring, and they are identifiable as stances in relation to the medium and a social other or others.

A pattern of shared consumption, such as that observed between roommates or romantic pairs, involves joint creation of the experience. Parallel consumption activity, or a together but separate style, can be seen as another form of coordination. For example, a roommate pair such as Margaret and Lillian establish reading time through the tendency to devote a particular hour each day to books. However, shared consumption, for example simultaneously listening to the same recording or watching television together, is more likely to result in shared conversation about the program. Shared interpretations can be observed and understood as a more obvious manifestation of patterns of coordination and co-orientation. Focus on patterns of conjoint activity leads to the understanding of positive focus of attention on both the medium and other persons or activities in the environment, instead of an individualized pattern taking account of only positive and negative attention to the medium. Examining audience activity as coordination allows the enumeration of stances that emerge in relation to others and with a communication medium.

Just as performance can be distinguished from competence in linguistic models, the act of media consumption should not be reduced to knowledge of the "language." More important, the performance/competence distinction allows the examination of the less-than-ideal audience member whose tastes are fickle, whose attention is fleeting, and whose comprehension cannot be assumed at any given time.

Chapter 9

Control and Selectivity

The assumption that much television use in long-term care is nonselective is pervasive among caregivers. The tendency for those in long-term care to adopt a pattern of heavy, habitual television viewing raises the question of the degree to which television use is under the control of nursing home residents, or if it is largely reactive to the institutional environment. Television use is widely perceived to be nonselective if it is not particularly driven by taste preferences or content-specific motives. This chapter refutes that assumption, suggesting that one means of control that operates in response to institutional constraints is the adoption of media routines, some of which can be seen as strategies adopted by nursing home residents to exert some control over everyday life. They are strategies that use the television, but where the television message has little impact on the motivations or the gratifications. Television's strategic use represents control in a place where little control is possible.

A sense of control, according to Tobin (1980), is essential to the achievement of stability, and the key to surviving the transition to long-term care. Control resides in the ability to exercise freedom of choice over some aspects of daily life, however mundane. Control in this context appears to operate individually through the perception that one has choices to make. In practice, control implicates the processes and limitations that influence individual media selections as well, processes that are frequently social in origin.

Estelle sums up the awareness of the relation between the need for routine and the desire for individual control. She also comments on the negative consequences that occur without a sense of control:

> We've got a program that we follow routinely. And it's so easy, you know? There's not a lot of stress. We get up in the

101

morning and we know exactly what we're gonna do for the rest of the day. Of course, any deviation, you know, throws us all out of kilter. Like going out, going shopping, that definitely throws us out of kilter.

Just pick your own routine and you feel you've got some kind of control over what's going on around you. Especially when you get into a place like this because you have so little control.

The field of selectivity encompasses nonmedia activities as well as media use. As the passage above indicates, shopping is one option that is limited for Estelle, as it is for most of the residents. Nonmedia routines influence media selectivity by limiting some options and rendering others more attractive. For Eileen, if shopping is an option that is constrained, it has implications for her media preferences. She says:

I read 'most all of the newspaper, but the ads are one thing I don't. Well, I don't go anywhere or buy anything anymore. Like I have to tell them, "Bill get something for me."

The limits of financial resources are not the only constraints operating here. Eileen is also limited in her ability to travel outside of the facility, and also by the spatial limitations of her shared room that do not allow for the accumulation of many personal possessions. But Eileen feels fortunate in that she has an attentive son who can provide the few purchases she needs. She depends on him, she says, for her favorite hand cream, suitable clothing, and the magazines that otherwise would not be available to her. If she did not have such an attentive son, she says she would have to do without them, as the rest of the residents without the same resources as Eileen must.

Since the ability to employ resources to meet desired ends is the minimum requirement to accomplish strategic manipulation of the environment, assessment of resources is an essential first step in comprehending the action premises that underlie the performance of media routines. In this way, disadvantaged nursing home residents are best described as those who have few resources to employ. Resources that Eileen has include control over time and space, money, possessions, mobility, friends, and knowledge. Establishing daily routines that are strategic in nature is how residents are able to exercise any degree of control over their lives in a place where such choices are limited to a narrow range of options.

One means of assessment of the limitations on individual control involves examining the constraints of time and space that create a structure of availability built around other necessary routines. These necessary routines include meals, naps, medical procedures, and personal care, and they determine the temporal and spatial availability for media consumption as well as other activities. Because Eileen can predict fairly well how her day will progress, she is free to plan, however minimally, the events of her day.

Eileen credits the fact that she is only mildly incontinent compared to others in the facility. She says she is mobile enough to get back to her room quickly when she has to, which allows her the freedom to roam. She schedules bathing and physical therapy as she does her hair appointments, and does not require regular time-consuming daily treatments, or sedatives that would further erode her free time. Using her wheelchair as a walker most of the time, she also likes maintaining the option to be pushed back quickly to her room if she has an accident that needs immediate attention.

Strategic manipulation depends not only on having resources, but also on one's ability to employ the resources that are available. To illustrate the point, consider the achievement of privacy, which is mentioned frequently by residents as a major source of dissatisfaction. Privacy violations are inevitable for individuals faced with frequent intrusions. But for couples who wish any level of intimacy, privacy is described as essential but nearly impossible in the nursing home. Privacy largely involves the ability and opportunity to manipulate living space. Assisted sometimes by the privacy curtains and lighting, the cooperation of others, and the positioning of furniture, the television set tends to be used as a barrier that includes intimates and excludes others.

The narratives also indicate that privacy is an accomplishment of negotiation with staff, relatives, and roommates. These negotiations implicate other resources such as communication faculties and status or some other leverage.

The use of television to create private space is essential to many nursing home residents, who cite the ability to drown out unpleasant sounds and transcend the immediate environment as characteristic privacy strategies. The strategic aspects of Dan and Gerry's domestic routine is evident in their account of the environment outside of their room:

> D: We don't go out there. I don't know, I just go out there to smoke. We go to the dining room and go back here and that's about the size of it. You feel so much empathy for the people in here, you know, that they can walk out of their rooms immediately.
>
> G: And they don't know where they're at.
>
> D: And maybe be six inches from their rooms and they don't know where they're at. And I have empathy for them, but the thing of it is that I don't want to see it because I may be that way someday myself. So, I'd rather not deal with it if I can get out of it, you know. Rather than to start dealing with it now. So, like I say, we watch TV. That's our main entertainment.

It is important to note that the use of television to create privacy is prevalent, and it is accomplished in several ways. The option to create privacy or to relocate to another space are both employed depending on the resources available. The option to inhabit the public television lounges seems to be gender inflected as well, since it is rarely taken up by the women of Hilltop at all unless entertaining guests. Women tend to gather in the kitchen-like atmosphere of the activity room, open only during certain hours of the day, and supervised by activity department personnel. Women generally do not go by themselves to the lounges to just get out of their rooms, watch television, visit, and perhaps smoke, but the men do so frequently. The women tend to find other ways of establishing their own space. As Eileen mentions, her strategy is to draw the curtain separating the two sides of the room while turning on the television. This creates two different, gender-inflected strategies of attaining privacy. One style requires the mobility to claim a public space, and the other is a style more characterized by the ability to withdraw into one's own private space.

Establishing one's own routines requires the understanding of the rhythms and the limits of institutional life, identification of needs and desires, and the ability to strategically maximize available resources toward meeting those needs. Residents unable to establish reliable routines experience shifting care priorities, or are unable to recognize or anticipate their daily needs. But those who do are better able to cope with the environment. They are able to thrive largely through the ability to carve out a personal space in an otherwise impersonal place.

Residents who thrive are better able to maximize resources and adapt their social routines to the institutional rhythm if they can recognize opportunities and define them as familiar problems. Interviews suggest that some previously learned practices assist in strategically adapting to the routines of institutional life. This allows new social routines to develop within previously established frames, but with common strategic goals unique to the institutional context.

Dan's personal history of fierce independence reveals his difficulty adapting to the nursing home was due to the personal freedom to which he had become accustomed:

> When you find ways to control your movement and the way you do things, it makes you feel a little bit better about yourself because you've got something going for you. It's better than just sitting around and waiting for someone to come along and tell you you've got to do this, and you've got to do that, and this has got to be done now. That's why I was a truck driver. You made the job what you wanted it to be. If you wanted to make a lot of money, then you could make a lot of money. If you didn't care about making a lot of money, then you could have more recreational time. But you set your own pace which gave you control. It's sort of like being self-employed.

For Dan, then, institutional living presents the familiar problem of "setting your own pace," or establishing a routine, which he equates with gaining control. Although his present circumstances represent significant changes from the lifestyle of the truck driver he once inhabited, he applies a familiar frame of reference to his current situation. Having established a work pattern that was "like being self-employed," he recognizes the value of predictable routines to maximize free time.

Douglas and Isherwood (1979) discuss the relation between daily routine and consumption periodicity, arguing that high frequency, nonpostponable routines tend to cluster such that there is a relation between one's work patterns and time available for leisure pursuits. Although not generally engaged in productive labor, nursing home residents are subject to high-frequency demands that operate like work demands and are not easily coordinated with low-frequency, longer duration leisure activities. The ability to adjust to high-frequency demands may be related to consistency with rhythms of periodicity developed earlier in life.

Dan, for example, whose work history was suggested previously, has had to accommodate high-frequency care demands and other constraints that represent changes in the "work" portion of his day. Because he has been accustomed to a much greater degree of control over everyday life, the transition to long-term care was particularly difficult for him. Through changes in his media routines, he maintains some consistency with his former life by exerting more control over his available time. His media routines reflect this level of control in the amount of time he spends planning and preparing for media consumption, spending time each day reading *TV Guide*, ordering videotapes by mail, and seeking out movies and programs to record on his VCR for later use.

In addition to time constraints, spatial considerations place limitations on nursing home activities as well. Spatial constraints include the physical limitations that determine the extent and range of possible motion, and routine nursing home scheduling practices that limit out-of-facility travel options. Both of these constraints are physical factors of embodiment. Although some of the nursing home residents are able to measure their range of motion in miles, especially with friends and relatives who provide opportunities for outings, most are limited to movement within or between rooms. The the field of activity selection is necessarily limited to within this circumscribed range.

Residents speak of the occasional field trip outside of the nursing home as desirable, but they are extremely difficult to organize and rare. Just as Estelle and Eileen rarely leave the facility to shop because they find it disruptive to the daily routine, Clark talks about the reasons he rarely goes fishing anymore even though he still enjoys it and the facility sometimes organizes an excursion:

> Oh every so often they have a bus out here. They load up a bus load and take you around, oh different places, oh maybe down to the lake. I don't do too much of that on account of they have to lift you up. They got a lift, and drop that down and wheel me up onto that short van. But not very often. Too much trouble.

Although each exerts its own particular demands, constraints of time and space tend to work together such that one who travels slowly can cover less ground in a given time. Residents with only a short period of time between nonpostponable activities can only be available to travel a short distance. Interviews yield many instances where the distinction between time and space is blurred because residents tend to measure the distance between points in terms of the time it takes to travel there. Such blurring is evident in one resident's account of why she never ventures outside the nursing home:

> Like Chester, he can go out and run around (the home) on a nice day, but unless somebody pushes me, that's quite a long while.

The amount of time spent in media consumption in the nursing home can best be explained not in terms of the gross amount of leisure time available, but in terms of a structure of availability responsive to the high-frequency demands placed on residents. Although a resident may have eight hours of "free time" in a day and may spend all eight hours reading and watching television, routine demands limit the duration of each individual media interaction to an hour or less. Due to frequent interruptions by meals, naps, and medical procedures, investing large blocks of time in any given activity is difficult or altogether impossible. But for some residents, that represents more of a loss than for others. Generally the men seem to place greater value on the ability to go outside. They talk about it more frequently, and have devised a variety of related strategies.

The spatial limitations imposed by individual physical mobility and scheduled institutional activity limit travel options. These limitations work together to place the nursing home residents in, or close to, their rooms most of the time. Consumption choices tend to strategically maximize limited temporal resources while minimizing physical energy output.

In the nursing home, the creation of the illusion of space is as important as the actual physical context. Television choices provide a form of vicarious mobility and a constant source of difference and stimulation in a world that does not otherwise change very much. Rowles' (1978) ethnography of older adults' use of space highlights the importance of contrasting past and present uses of space in order to understand how limitations of mobility are strategically overcome. He argues that watching the movement of others is an important way that the aged counter the sense of restriction.

Both live and mediated examples of vicarious mobility can be found in the nursing home. Clark, for example, who misses activities such as theater and fishing excursions, talks about why he likes to sit in the hall across from the nurses' station while listening to the radio. "There's always something, some activity going on so I spend quite a bit of time down at the office here." He says, however, that he is just as likely to turn on the television set as he is to observe the nursing station activity. In fact most days he does both. Although he is one of the busier residents, engaging in more different activities in a day than most, he has long been accustomed to a busy lifestyle. He says he is surprised at how little he does in a day now.

> Thinking back a long time to what I used to do in my younger days, I wonder how in the world I ever done that. Now I'm not doing anything some days. I used to work 10, 12, 15 hours a day or more, then go home and go to a picture show or this or that and the other. Get home at 1:00, get up at 6:00 in the morning. Didn't think anything about it.

Although Clark recognizes the important differences in his lifestyle these days, his media choices reflect his busy former life. However, most of the activities he engages in are daily routines which to him feel like "not doing anything some days."

He tends to move from one activity to another frequently throughout his day, beginning with the radio when he first wakes up and morning television until breakfast. He spends several hours each day reading the newspaper, magazine articles, and short stories. He changes activities frequently, rarely spending more than thirty minutes engaged in any one pursuit. It is typical to observe him reading a magazine for a while, watching a television program, picking up a book for twenty minutes, and then taking a portable radio on his wheelchair while he observes the activity at the nurses' station.

Bert's activities also reflect his former lifestyle while responding to the current demands of the institution. Because Bert is unable to coordinate with his roommate at all, he avoids evening television consumption altogether, preferring the early morning hours when there are fewer distractions:

> I'm usually in bed before 8:00, and most days I get up at 4:00 in the morning. I come in here (the lounge) and watch this one. I get more out of it you see. I get the weather channel on and whatever's going on, you know, and hardly any of the aides are here. They're out working most of the time. So I enjoy TV at that time of the morning pretty good, you know. Everything's quiet. I don't like a lot of noise when I'm watching TV.

Bert finds the early morning hours more pleasurable for television consumption because, as he says, there are fewer distractions at that hour. Bert prefers old movies, especially westerns, but finds that the time and space for the concentration necessary to enjoy them present certain obstacles, not the least of which is an unstable roommate situation. Thus, he has established a routine that accommodates his preferences and his roommate situation, and he integrates his preferences strategically with routine demands of the institution.

Because he spent more than forty years of his life farming, Bert says he has always been able to rise early in the morning. However, he used to stay up much later in the evening. He says when television was a relatively new phenomenon in the late 1950s and early 1960s, he developed a habit of staying up late at night watching television, particularly during the winter months when he had fewer work responsibilities. Given a choice between morning and evening hours, he now expresses a strong preference for the early morning hours. He has combined two patterns developed when he was younger—the tendency to rise early and the tendency to watch television by himself while the rest of the household slept. Years of farming allowed him to establish a certain pattern of consumption periodicity, with high-frequency constraints characterizing the busy part of his year and leaving no available leisure time. The summer pattern is offset by low-frequency demands in the winter that allow for a different winter consumption pattern. Low frequency in this context does not mean less overall time. On the contrary, it means that time is available for longer periods of consumption, a pattern associated with a particular work schedule and suggestive of higher status.

Douglas and Isherwood (1979) argue that low-frequency work demands are associated with low-frequency, higher status consumption patterns, allowing greater flexibility and freedom from nonpostponable tasks. Although farm life in summer can be characterized as high-frequency demand, the winter months provide a model of a more leisured lifestyle if summer harvests yield enough resources to sustain the winter. According to Bert, part of the pleasure he used to derive from late-night television consumption came from a sense of empowerment he felt. The empowerment derived from the ownership of a television set, the free time to enjoy it, and in his sense of pride in presiding over a successful economic enterprise that allowed a season of leisure.

> It was like I was lord of the manor, you know? It was just black and white. I didn't have no color. But I really enjoyed that thing. I set up all night til it went off'n the air.

Bert's use of early morning hours recreates a sense of his leisure patterns of the past. This is accomplished through manipulation of his schedule and strategically using the available space. By reducing the amount of time he interacts with his roommate and making the most out of the lounge area, he also enhances his sense of competence. This point is important to discussion of his status in the facility, and his beliefs about the importance of appearance to him.

Where mobility is the key to a sense of control over space, Bert manages to preside over the lounge, which counters the lack of control he experiences in his room. He spends quite a bit of his time watching television across from his room in the smoker's lounge, the place where the men at Hilltop are likely to gather later in the day whenever the nurses have not designated the space for cartoons. However, in the early hours of the morning, the space belongs exclusively to him.

Parenthetically, the only television program preference trend that strictly follows gender lines is that the 42 percent (eleven) of the group who regularly watch soap operas are all women and the 27 percent (seven) of the group who watch television sports are all men. When compared only against members of their own sex, 69 percent of the women say they watch soap operas, and 70 percent of the men say they watch television sports.

The pattern of soap opera consumption can be seen to fit within the high-frequency, nonpostponable routines that characterize a domestic lifestyle. The work pattern of childcare and housework leaves short periods of time available for media consumption. Although Estelle claims to have developed an "addiction" to soap operas only recently, most of the women who watch soap operas on television say they developed an interest in them years ago. Several mention an interest in soap operas that dates back to when radio was the primary medium in the home and they were establishing themselves as young wives and mothers.

Sports events, however, are more characteristic of low-frequency demands. They are scheduled less often than soap operas, and each event is longer in duration. Sports events fit within a work schedule that accommodates longer periods of leisure activity, less often.

Consider, for example, the two roommates, Clark and Charlie. During their afternoon ball game, neither of them is able to stay awake from the beginning to the end of the game. This behavior can perhaps be explained in terms of the energy requirements to return to their room after lunch, or it can be explained in terms of the routine requirement of sleep at that particular time of day. However, a more complete explanation considers the intersection of routines and the way the two men coordinate their consumption practice with each other, and within their physical boundaries. When asked how they spent the afternoon, both account for that time in terms of the media event rather than in terms of the nap it accommodates. Their content choice, a sports event, can be seen as a strategic choice in response to current physical demands because televised sports events are in a media genre that can be appreciated without having to attend to the whole game. On the other hand, it can also be seen as a strategic choice that allows them to minimize their need for sleep by letting them recount their primary activity as watching the ball game.

Although preferences for soap operas and sports events may be established earlier in life, they are accommodated differently into the nursing home routine. Superficially they can be seen as a difference represented only at the content level. However, they continue to maintain a more fundamental gender and status difference, even though the work demands that may have inscribed the difference have largely disappeared.

Soap operas are highly repetitive, daily routines that frequently serve as accompaniments to other tasks. In the nursing home, craft activities and housekeeping often accompany soap operas, and soap operas are considered low-priority routines by both staff and the residents who adhere to them. Consequently, consumption routines are characterized by high levels of interruption and correspondingly low levels of attention.

Soap opera viewers leave the program on while they participate in interview sessions, sometimes lowering the volume and sometimes not. In apparent contradiction to Margaret's rules for domestic viewing, she keeps her television set tuned to one of her soap operas throughout the interview session. During that same interview session, she tells me:

> And another thing, if the TV is on and we have company, the TV is shut off. I will not have that TV blaring. I've had very close friends that I refuse to visit because you go in and they still have to watch that TV. If I want to watch TV I can sit at home and watch TV. I don't have to go somewhere else to do it. If you're going to have company you're going to talk to them, not listen to that.

Perhaps, for her, turning down the sound is equivalent to turning off the set, but the apparent contradiction is reinforced in her eye behavior, as she continues to glance at the screen every so often, allowing it to mildly divert her attention. The contradiction may be resolved for her by considering that the interviewer is not "company," but a part of the routine of the nursing home. But she is also distinguishing between different modes of television consumption. For her, monitoring an afternoon soap opera during an unscheduled, drop-in visit apparently does not constitute rudeness. But "having company," requires a different set of rules, rules that give primacy to conversation. For Margaret, then, there are apparently at least two modes of consumption, and and least two styles of visitation as well.

This is markedly different from the consumption patterns observed during the men's afternoon sporting events. The relative importance of a ball game may be tied to its periodicity. Because it occurs less often than a soap opera, more importance is attached to it. But the behavioral difference observed is not strictly gendered behavior for all television because this event elicits different behavior than other programs like news or game shows that the men also enjoy. The men's sports viewing behavior follows a different set of rules and requires different levels of attention. The men are reluctant to turn down the sound or divide their attention during a game, unless they fall asleep. Conversation not related to the games is strictly confined to commercial breaks. No real interviewing could occur during these events.

While simultaneously occurring in different rooms, soap operas tend to be viewed solitarily or in domestic pairs, while sports television tends to attract more viewers, and visitors are welcome. The only public area where soap operas are seen is the kitchen-like activity room, while any of the public lounges might also gather a male sports crowd. Considering that women in the facility outnumber the men by more than three to one, the tendency for men to dominate the public areas emphasizes the relation between gender and space.

Strategic choices made by residents in the scheduling of events reflect the influence of the rhythms of patterns of activity established earlier in life, such as gendered behavior, as well as the ever-present routines of nursing home life. Scheduling reflects different levels of interest and valuation, and a different use of public space. Not all choices occur on the same plane. The more active residents say that they choose activities to fill free time after first mentally blocking out the times that they must be doing something else, a process that is evident in conversations about activity planning. Use of the activity schedule illustrates the activity selection process. The schedule indicates the placement various media choices hold in relation to other activities.

Residents who use the activity schedule tend to consult it when it is distributed at the beginning of each month and look for special events such as guest speakers, visiting musicians, and field trips. Events that are considered special have a connection to the world outside of the facility. Although fishing trips, like the one mentioned by Clark, or restaurant and shopping excursions enjoyed by Dan and Gerry may be rare, the appearance of a guest speaker or performer occurs once or twice each week. These are the best-attended nursing home activities, particularly for the women, who seem to prefer structured public activities.

Most of the residents who participate in scheduled activities look forward to the ones they consider special events as a diversion from the routine that is not too disruptive. Estelle, for example, knows the church affiliations and names of all the clergy expected in a given month, since she considers activities with religious affiliation to be the most pleasurable. Residents say they feel comfortable planning special events a month or so into the future, but not much more than this. According to Eileen, "I couldn't remember more than a month at a time, and besides, who knows if I'll still be here next month?" The calendar is typically consulted again to plan events by the week, and in the morning to plan activity attendance of the day. This scheduling process reveals a preference hierarchy of low-frequency special events, regular weekly events, and daily routines, with daily routines taken for granted and not given much special consideration.

Media consumption can be seen to follow a similar pattern. Estelle says, for example, that she would gladly miss any number of routine events to stay in her room and watch a program featuring Billy Graham on television. She considers this type of television program a special media event that is second only to a church service or some other activity with visiting clergy.

Activity calendars, then, a useful marker of the periodicity of activity participation, are a common sight on bedside tables. By the end of the month, it is easy to see signs of wear indicating frequent consultation among those who use them. Estelle is one of the residents who uses the activity calendar to plan her time. She reads the calendar for the week as though it only shows the activities that are interesting or important to her:

> Now on Mondays you go down to get your fingernails cleaned and painted. And on Tuesday we have Bible Study. And on Wednesday we have Bingo. And on Thursday we have a Ladies' Circle—that's another church meeting—and on Friday it's donuts and *Wheel of Fortune*. They want you to go down there where we sat this morning in the activity room and watch it. Then on Saturdays they have movies. Saturday afternoon at the movies, and ice cream. The ice cream parlor is open every day except Wednesday.

Estelle's use of the activity calendar is typical, and she chooses to focus her participation on one activity per day, planning her day around it and perhaps adding a trip to the ice cream parlor or the gift shop before returning to her room. Her activity calendar also doubles as a bookmark for her *TV Guide*. After she consults the activity calendar in the morning, she checks the television listings to look for what she considers to be special programming. With meals and essential routines providing a basic structure for her day, she fills the rest of her day with craft activities and routine events that include the newspaper, soap operas, and game shows.

Not all residents avail themselves of scheduled activities, however. Dan and Gerry, for example, are among those who avoid the scheduled activities altogether. They consider themselves to be of a different generation than most of the residents, and it is important to them that their activities be age-appropriate. They prefer each other's company, they say, but they are also responding to extremely high-frequency care demands. Outside of essential routines, Dan and Gerry structure their day entirely with television. Dan explains their schedule:

> At ten o'clock I'll get up and go out. And they'll see me on the cart [his scooter] so they'll know that we're up. And the nurse will be right there and she comes right on in and takes care of her. Then we watch Geraldo Rivera and by the time they get her out it's time for *The Price is Right*. Then we go down for dinner and we watch the noon news on 13. And then we get up

at quarter to four and we watch *Highway to Heaven* and at five o'clock we watch *Entertainment Tonight*. The only time that changes from day to day is on weekends.

Selectivity can be seen to operate differently within the temporal and spatial demands of the nursing home. Residents choose their activities strategically in order to maximize their available resources, structuring their availability with activities chosen from a preference hierarchy that includes media events. With media use responding to various care demands, residents integrate different routines that evolve from different pasts. As they exhibit variety in individual consumption styles, residents also exhibit control and selectivity individually in ways that show a fairly rigid adherence to gender roles. They are motivated by the desire for similar outcomes of privacy, control, and self-expression.

Because limitations that residents experience tend to occur in both temporal and spatial realms, they are strategically countered with media and other social routines that serve to minimize losses. Media time frames are established in coordination with the rhythm of the facility and respond to individual preferences that have evolved over time. Physical limitations are countered by maximizing the sense of physical involvement, perhaps by watching active others.

Past experience also can be seen to influence media content choices through inscribing individuality such as the way gender differences are socially constructed. While the pressure that daily routine exerts is a more immediate and common influence in the institution, residents use different routines to counter what they perceive as negative about everyday life in the nursing home. The next chapter addresses some of the media strategies adopted in order to coordinate with others, and to minimize what they see as negative in the nursing home.

Chapter 10

Minimizing the Negatives

Nursing home residents exercise control over their lives through adopting strategies that counter what they perceive as negative about the environment. Citing the poor quality of institutional foods and lack of peer companionship as negatives, for example, Dan and Gerry talk about missing some of their favorite former activities now that they live in the nursing home. When one has an opportunity to leave the facility, as they do on occasion to visit a doctor, they go together and they try to combine the errand with something pleasurable to offset the discomforts, like going out to a movie or to lunch. Dan explains the obstacles to this strategy:

> But you know usually we're so pushed for time when we go out. She's got to lay down at 2:30 in the afternoon. So we have to go out between 11:00 and 2:30. Sometimes you just can't get those kinds of (doctor) appointments. And a lot of theatres and restaurants we like are, are just not suitable for handicapped. So I guess you could call us recluses.

Dan and Gerry are rarely able to fit a restaurant trip or a movie into their schedule. However, they can stop at a store to stock their refrigerator with supplements to their institutional diet, and they can buy videotapes for use in their VCR.

Although they are not entirely satisfied with the compromise, Dan and Gerry say they are making the most of the choices available to them. Perhaps more important, they derive a sense of pleasure from their ability to thwart the institutional routines by creating their own domestic routines in their shared room. Domesticity, for them, resides in their use of space and their possessions. Dan says this:

> It's like I say. We've got a refrigerator, a VCR, and we've got a popcorn popper. We've even got a coffeemaker down there and sometimes we use it. So we've got, really, all the things we need right here.

Because media consumption intersects with so many other everyday practices, it is useful to consider some of the more common routines that structure its availability and contribute to its meaning. Media use in the nursing home involves the intersection of the practices of food consumption, drug use, and the routines related to physical embodiment of the residents, which for many includes frequent periods of rest and toilet assistance. For those who are cognitively aware, public interaction bears the considerable risks of public embarrassment as well. The reality of restricted movement requires a dependency on others in order to simply move from place to place, a constraint that clearly interferes with activity selection, since selectivity assumes a freedom to enter and exit the media environment at will.

Sleep patterns are affected by both the widespread use of sedatives and other factors related to the pace and routine of institutional life. Nursing home policy dictates an appropriate time to go to bed at night and to get up in the morning, when to take meals, and when medical routines are scheduled. All of these factors exert their influence over media consumption practices. They limit availability and the level of possible involvement, and they introduce forces that help shape expectations of the kind of interaction that can occur.

Understanding the burden of embodiment for nursing home residents is essential to analysis of media experience from the resident's point of view. As the previous sections demonstrate, rules about appropriateness intersect with constraints of the body. Together they influence the degree to which media involvement can occur, in both public and private spaces. However, the constraints imposed do more than interfere with reception of media. They structure the event, ultimately influencing content preferences and the quality of interaction with others. The impact of these constraints is evident in the stances the nursing home audience members assume in relation to each other and to the medium.

The weekly movie routine illustrates the intersection of media use with nonmedia practices and suggests the strategic nature of participation in media-centered social events. It also addresses some of the problems in administrating such an event for an activity director, and the problems the residents encounter in attempting to derive benefits from attending public events.

At Hilltop, movies are shown one afternoon each week, using a portable VCR and 25-inch monitor set up in one corner of the dining room. The event is listed in the monthly calendar and through placement of a poster at the entrance of the dining hall during breakfast and lunch on the day of the event. In addition, the activity staff actively solicit participation through oral reminders throughout the day. Despite these attempts to create interest in the movies, there are typically fewer than ten people who come to the events under their own power. The rest of the audience is gathered by the activity staff, who go from room to room to ask residents individually if they would like to participate. Others, unable to respond, are wheeled in without securing their consent. The process of gathering residents together takes at least thirty minutes, during which time the early arrivals tend to get restless. The event usually begins before all the participants have arrived.

The movies are scheduled on weekend afternoons, around 2:00, or at least an hour after lunch. A few residents stay in the dining room at the end of the meal to wait for the event to begin, because it requires too much energy to leave and then return. Others need to return to their rooms in the interim. Just as some are not present at the beginning of the event, there are few left by the end. Some wish to be returned to their rooms early and ask to be wheeled out before the movie ends. Some doze off and then wake up and resume interest in the event. It is rare for anyone to be present and engaged for the entire activity, but perhaps twenty-five or thirty residents will significantly participate.

Because most cannot be present or attentive to the entire film and interruptions are frequent, preferences in movie selections reflect these restrictions. Familiar, older films with strong visual appeal such as *Gone with the Wind,* Disney animation, slapstick comedies such as the Abbott and Costello films, and popular musicals are among the favorites. The films most appreciated are those that require little concentration to plot and character development and can be appreciated during short periods of engagement.

Consider the movie experience when a film that violates those criteria is shown, from the point of view of an eighty-year-old long-term resident named Ruth. Ruth is catheterized for urinary incontinence and is dependent on the nursing staff to change the reservoir every day after lunch. She is lucky if she does not have to wait. As soon as she is free, she returns to the dining room for the movie since it is one of her favorite activities. As she wheels herself into the darkened dining room, the video screen is filled with chaotic images of a man and a neoadolescent boy cavorting with an aerosol can of Silly String. The film, *Big*, has already begun, and Ruth has missed the essential premise of the movie.

Later she shares her impressions. She was not sure when she arrived how much time had elapsed since the film started. She tried to concentrate, for it was unusual to her that it was a film she did not immediately recognize. She winced at every shriek and giggle in the scene and looked to see if any of the eight or ten others in attendance shared her opinion. When one character pretended that the aerosol substance was shooting from his nose, Ruth loudly expressed disgust, but no one responded to her criticism. Four were engaged in conversation and did not seem to notice. Two others were dozing, including Phyllis, who often shares Ruth's point of view, and two appeared to be interested in the film and paid no attention to Ruth's comments.

Ruth politely accepted a bag of popcorn that her teeth would not allow her to eat, dispensed by Angie, the new young assistant in the activity department, who has stopped trying to explain the beginning of the movie she chose. After one more display of boyish antics on the screen, Ruth again looked to Phyllis, who was still dozing. Then she wheeled herself out of the room into the activity room next door to peruse a magazine. Still unhappy about the movie choice, she looked for an opportunity to talk about it. She compared the relative value of the magazine article she chose to the offensive lessons she felt were offered in this week's film.

Ruth is somewhat unusual in that she is able to exercise choice by leaving the room. More than half of the residents are not as mobile. She is also articulate and reflective in accounting for her own behavior. She argues that she has a stake in the movie activity as a regular event and wants to be consulted in the movie selection. She says that she chose to leave the room after an unsatisfying experience with the movie, but in a lengthy conversation, she speculates that three conditions might have prolonged her stay. First, if she had been present at the beginning of the film, she might have appreciated the offensive scenes in context. Second, if someone else in the audience had recognized her response, she might have felt validated and continued her involvement. And third, if the snack had been something that she could have eaten, she might have at least stayed long enough to finish it, and perhaps become more involved in the plot.

However, the conditions that might have prolonged her stay are less significant to her than the criteria she advances for her choice to leave. And because she is partially mobile, she knows she can act on a critical appraisal of the film. Others who are less mobile rely on different strategies, such as engaging in conversation, waiting for someone to remove them, creating a disruptive outburst, or simply falling asleep.

The public nature of the movie event distinguishes it from the experience of privately viewing a television movie in one's own room. There are several conditions that render concentration more difficult in the public dining area. Many residents have some hearing loss, but there is also usually quite a bit of activity in the dining area creating competitive sounds. Attendants wheel residents in and out, the dining hall staff set the tables for the next meal, and the activity staff circulate, passing out snacks. Seating is constantly adjusted. Nurses enter with medications and exit with residents who require cleaning, rest, or treatment. Throughout the movie, conversation between residents continues, both related to the film and not.

Long stretches of film dialogue, then, are not well received. And the preference for familiar and visual films makes sense in light of the noise factors alone. But for most of the residents who come to the movies, it is not only the film but the social interaction that brings them. Residents with their own televisions can watch old movies with fewer interruptions in the privacy of their rooms, and those who want only conversation can gather in the lounges, the hallways, and the activity area.

The interaction renders the event unique because the film provides an ongoing stream of material for conversation. Often the conversations include references to the film and comments about the actors, costumes, and sets. Sometimes the comments are more personal in nature when the film evokes a memory or prompts recall of some past experience. One of the more important functions of the film is to promote such reminisence. And the activity director plays an important role in orchestrating the media events, not only determining which movie will be shown, but in prompting the conversation that ensues.

The difficulty of finding appropriate films is highlighted by Ruth's experience. But some long-term residents like Ruth are clear in their preferences and expectations. And because care facilities bring together people of widely disparate backgrounds and tastes, scheduling several smaller weekly sessions that appeal to different tastes instead of one large one is Ruth's suggestion for more successful movie events.

There is clearly a generation gap between the couple Gerry and Dan, discussed previously, who spend a lot of time privately with a VCR. But there is an even wider gulf between the couple, and Ruth or Phyllis. Both women are over eighty years old, and not nearly among the oldest residents. Although the residents over eighty generally show no interest in operating a VCR on their own, they like the structured public movie events, as long as someone else operates the machine. The fact that younger residents such as Dan are already more comfortable with the technology, suggests widespread familiarity is likely in the near future.

Staff members fill essential roles, bringing the residents where the event will occur, making decisions about who is capable or interested, and perhaps organizing any discussion that ensues. Yet the interaction that results belongs to the residents who respond with interest. The audience behaviors observed indicate the limits of control, particularly for women, over a public event. The motivations to participate vary, and the strategies that residents have at their disposal to counter the negatives are often limited as well.

Activity participation reflects the desire to be seen as competent, a result of the constant need for evaluation of resident behavior by care providers. But the motivation to cooperate with the routine of the facility and appear competent in public spaces does not seem to diminish the value of the spontaneous interaction to the participants. This event must also be seen as a rare opportunity for personal expression, particularly for the women who inhabit the public spaces rarely and more cautiously than the men.

Residents of the care facility do not exhibit wholesale signs of social withdrawal predicted with increased media use, and even withdrawal is shown to contain strategic dimensions. Media-centered activities, such as the movie event, are fundamentally social in nature, and appreciated as markedly different from private consumption, which is differently motivated. Even an instance that might be labeled as withdrawal, such as Phyllis falling asleep during parts of the film, can be interpreted as a strategic act involving the manipulation of a limited attention resource while attempting to derive the benefits of a public, structured event. The next section demonstrates media use strategies that further enhance self-expression and image by drawing on qualities such as notoriety and legitimacy that the media confer.

Chapter 11

Storytelling: Accentuating the Positive

Instances where media consumption serves strategic ends appear throughout this volume represented in accounts of goal-directed manipulation of resources that reveal some of the motives for media use. Bert's story shows that adaptation to the nursing home occurs through modifying previously learned practices and strategically adapting them to his present circumstances. Dan and Gerry feel they are able to exercise greater control over their available time by adopting strategies that employ their considerable shared resources to counter what they perceive as negative within the environment. Clark's tale illustrates how some residents are able to maximize limited time and energy by adopting a strategy of frequently changing activities. Eileen and Bert both employ different mobility strategies in order to escape the surroundings of their rooms, and construct their own social environments. The demonstration of competence, creation of couple status, and even the strategic use of media to induce sleep or to provide justification for constructive use of time are all in some way strategic manipulations.

The examples used thus far also demonstrate different opportunities for personal expression. Instances where media can be seen to be employed strategically provide the best opportunities to transcend space and time and create a sense of self that is not bound by the institutional context. Atchley (1989) argues that themes that form the basis for identity are necessary to create a transcendent sense of self. Continuity occurs through the ability to maintain a consistent self-image, despite external changes that modify behaviors. The ability to exercise media choices provides many opportunities for continuity between past life events and life in long-term care, but there are few opportunities for residents to create a sense of self that is not bound and defined by the institution.

In order to adopt a strategy, it is essential to envision some desired outcome and to have the means and the resources to manipulate the environment toward that end. However, as their accounts reveal, the residents profiled in this study are somewhat atypical from the general nursing home population in that they are privileged to be able to achieve some of those goals. In fact, what distinguishes all the resident narratives is that it shows they possess attributes that can be considered resources. From examination of their accounts, it is clear that this group has mobility, mental acuity, sensory faculties, knowledge, status, friends and loved ones, privacy, and available time. Media provide greater material benefits for those with the ability to use them, allowing media consumption itself, and particularly a diversity of media options, to be considered another valuable resource.

Within the nursing home, the most common complaints involve problems common to institutionalized living. The lack of privacy, loss of control over routines, impersonal treatment by the staff, limited personal possessions, and the constant presence of death, loss, and pain all are perceived as negatives that create serious obstacles. However, those with the resources to transcend some of these negatives experience adjustment and even comfort within the facility. The contributions of media consumption to this equation are unique.

Where material resources may be lacking, the ability to manipulate the media environment can also accomplish strategic enhancement of self. More specifically, the use of media stories is tactical performance of identity enhancement, providing evidence of a past self, signifying familial connectedness, and creating status relationships with others in the institution. What is common to these strategies is that they all serve to express something about the individual who uses them.

Residents may derive the most pleasure from media stories with an uplifting theme. Positive, moralistic tales, such as those featured in the popular television program *Highway to Heaven,* provide an ideal program type. Happy endings and inspirational messages help to lift spirits and elevate moods, but happy endings and success stories are not confined to the small screen. Instances where a story is employed outside the moment of consumption reveal something of the storytellers as well. Participation in success stories can mean identifying with and sharing a narrative derived from mass media. The narratives most often shared in this way tend to show triumph over adversity. Some examples illustrate how these stories have become part of the personal narratives, taken up because the tellers identify with some aspect of the tale.

Estelle, for example, most admires the story of Darrell Gilyard, a black minister who gained national exposure on Reverend Jerry Falwell's *Old-Time Gospel Hour*. In Gilyard's story of self-determination, he persevered to educate himself and overcame a homeless childhood. After saying on several occasions, "It's just like that colored minister fellow," Estelle finally tells the story, which turns into a parable for her own condition:

> His mother gave him up and after he got a little bit older he only lived underneath a bridge, and he stayed under there, and he went to school. He took care of himself, bought his own clothes. When he wanted to wash, they'd go right to the river and wash in river water. But he took care of his own self. When you have nobody to do anything, you do it yourself. Now he went to high school and college, and he's a minister. He's a nice looking colored boy. And he's married now and got a family of his own. He tells you about many things, you know, people who was crippled. One fellow on the TV Sunday, he was in a wheelchair with a leg taken off. And he said, "No sir, I want to be right where I'm at." And so do I. I been through about a million operations, but I'm still getting along pretty good though.

This success story told by Estelle begins with a story of the minister, and a first moral appears in the middle—"When you have nobody to do anything, you do it yourself." Then Estelle continues her tale about the minister, ending with a second lesson about satisfaction with one's lot in life. At this point, she turns the tale to draw a more obvious parallel with her own situation. She uses the story in two ways in her conversations. First she uses it to illustrate her self-sufficiency, where being in the nursing home represents independence from reliance on her family, with whom relations are largely strained. Then she uses it to illustrate the importance in having faith and not wanting more than you have. On another occasion she says this:

> The Doctor says, Doctor Wagner asked me when I got my hip broke, he had me on the walker and then on the cane. After I left my cane home he said, "What'd you do with your cane?" I said I left the darn thing home. He said, "I wish all my patients could be like you." But you see this leg here, see I can straighten this up like that, but this knee here I can't. This is about as far as I can get. The doctor says too many fractures in that one leg. He told me this knee is frozen. So that's why that leg is bigger than this one. Way bigger. But I can do for myself. They don't have to push me around 'cause I can do for my own self. Just like that colored minister boy.

An example from conversations with Margaret takes a similar turn. When telling me about herself and her family, she inserts a story about a media event to illustrate her point. Although she appears to be handling her recent confinement to a wheelchair fairly well, her identification with a pair of media events might suggest otherwise. She begins the tale by talking about missing family gatherings and, in general, things which are currently out of her control:

> We just more or less do whatever we want to when we want to. Except now. I think we'll be doing it when my leg says we can.

However, she appears to have wandered from the point, and she begins drawing heavily from the story of Jessica McClure, the little girl who fell into a drain pipe in 1987, which resulted in a dramatic rescue with heavy media coverage. Coming toward the end of her story, Margaret draws a third parallel to another drama that she witnessed in the early 1920s. Then she returns to a conversation about herself:

> I think the one I remember more was Floyd Collins. He was trapped in a cave down by Mammoth Caves. Of course that was not too far from where I lived. We listened to that night

and day. He did finally die. They were not able to rescue him, but we listened to that night and day. That was going on for days. We just couldn't get away from that radio. But that little girl made it. Thank the Lord. It just shows you. And I guess now we won't be doing too much dancing. Because of my leg. But I'll make it.

This story can be read as a statement about faith in God in times of adversity, or it can be read as a story about perseverance. Although Margaret does not explicitly state what the moral of this story is for her, her statement, "It just shows you," indicates that for her, the point of the story is self-evident.

Her telling of the story occurred several years after the rescue of Jessica McClure and sixty-five or more years after the failed attempt to rescue Floyd Collins. Yet, Margaret sees these stories as important parables for her experience, and worth relating. Her meaning may be somewhat obscure, but she uses the stories as a way to relate to a relative stranger. She offers common media ground to bridge the distance between us and illustrates her point with a story she expects is already known.

In addition to general stories that serve as parables for those who use them, there are also personal stories circulated in the institution that perform identity maintainance for some of the residents. Storytelling, in this case, is a mode of personal expression that places the user in a central position as both storyteller and character in a story that may be taken up by others. The purpose of such stories may be to create a sense of self as hero, as recipient of favors, or as central to meeting the needs of others. While others have investigated storytelling in the nursing home (Unruh, 1983), what is unique about the involvement of media in modes of personal expression is the added legitimacy accorded media-related events. These stories function strategically to counter some of the negative aspects of institutionalization. Through their use, something can be inferred about the values of the storyteller as well as the aspects of institutionalization that the storyteller wishes to counter.

Because the nursing home tends to homogenize the residents into a group devoid of personality and individuality, probably the most common strategic ploy is to carve a distinctive identity that enhances the image and status of the teller. Maintaining that image requires the occasional retelling of the story in addition to exhibiting behavior that remains consistent with the image of self projected in the story.

For example, Clark readily admits that he seeks to maintain a worldly image of himself despite the fact that his world has become increasingly small since entering the facility. He holds the dubious distinction of having been in the institution longer than anyone currently living there. However, his status is compromised by his inability to meet former activity levels and his displeasure at his image, particularly the current state of his wardrobe. His clothes are always clean, and he takes care with his personal grooming, but he laments the facts that he is no longer very stylish, his clothes need mending, and they do not fit him very well anymore.

He counters some of the distress resulting from the lack of consistency between his past and present selves by reminding others of his past, his former good looks, and how others responded to his appearance. He does not have to tell his best story often because others maintain the image. However, when asked, he happily relates his tale, embellished with lavish detail and obvious enjoyment. Wishing the story to emerge unprompted, interview questions did not reveal to Clark that his story had been told by others, although by the time he was interviewed, there were five field note references where others had told all or part of his story. When he did choose to tell it, he appeared eager, his eyes brightened, and he leaned forward nearly out of his seat. About thirty minutes into the first interview session, the topic shifted from his reading habits to film. Without answering the question he was asked, he launched into his story, which took about ten minutes to tell, without interruption.

Clark's opening came when he was asked what kinds of movies he used to like, to which he responds:

> Oh I'm just trying to remember. There's one lady that always went with me.

After four sentences to establish what he was doing at that time of his life, he reveals the name of his date:

> She'd come down to see the records and sheet music we had in the basement. And her name was Mae West.

At this point in the story, Clark switches to the more practiced lines of the story, settling back in his chair and smiling throughout. He describes how they met in 1926, and how she pursued him from city to city when he frequently changed jobs during that period of his life, a period that lasted about twenty years:

> So I went to East Saint Louis and I got a call she'd be down the following Thursday, that she'd be in to see me. Same way every store I was in up and down the East Coast. She found out I went to Hoboken, came down to see me and wanted me to have dinner with her. About the same way when I finally got around to Chicago or Connecticut. She made sure I had her address.

Clark's story also contrasts his casual attitude about dating someone famous with the reactions of others when she would contact him:

> They called me to go up to the office, and I went up. They said, "You won't believe it, you won't believe it, you won't believe it." I said, "What?" She said, "Mae West is calling you!" I said, "Oh, okay." So she said that she'd be down the following Thursday, and I never thought anything about it. I went down and told my employees, and they told everybody that they knew. Come Thursday at 11:00, I had to get the boys out of the basement to get the people out of the road so she could get in the store.

Clark's telling of the story places himself in the center, pursued by a woman who was both beautiful and famous. Because she is a well-known persona, Mae West's image enhances Clark's status by association, yet it allows him to remain aloof from the story with the narrative point of view he chooses. His description of the reaction of his fellow employees, and the commotion caused by one of her visits, shows that she was interested in Clark when she was at the height of her popularity. He dates the period from 1926 until around World War II to emphasize this point.

The story is a useful strategy because it serves to bring Clark a measure of celebrity status. Also, the fact that others willingly tell the tale for him shows that it is an effective strategy. The tale also gives him status as an expert on Hollywood at that point in time. People respond to this role by asking him questions about prewar movies relatively often. The story he tells influences his current media consumption routines in a significant way, since he is expected to maintain consistency through continuing his interest in Mae West in the nursing home. He is informed, particularly by his male friends, whenever someone notices a Mae West picture is being shown on television. Then Clark is expected to watch the films and provide them with inside information about the actress.

Others in the nursing home have celebrity tales to tell as well. Another resident tells of an acquaintance relationship with Lawrence Welk, and one tells a story of meeting Franklin D. Roosevelt. However, none of the tales have exactly the same impact. This is partly due to the nature of the relationship Clark and Mae West shared, since they were more than acquaintances. It is also partly due to his expert telling of the story that downplays his role while simultaneously enhancing his image in the institution.

Eileen also has a story that uses media legitimation to contribute to a celebrity image, but hers has a more recent origin. Her tale allows her to integrate events from her past while simultaneously allowing an enhancement of her present status in the facilty. Based on information from an interview with a reporter from a local weekly newspaper in 1990, Eileen was featured in a full-page cover story as a participant in the women's movement. The reporter was looking for sources who remembered the passage of the Nineteenth Amendment, which granted women the right to vote in April of 1920. Eileen was nineteen and a newlywed at the time the amendment passed. Ironically, she says she did not care one way or another about the amendment at the time. Not being old enough to vote in that first election, she says she was more concerned about being married than being politically active. However, she had two aunts who were active suffragettes—a dirty word locally at the time—and over time the event has come to have greater significance for Eileen as a family story. Being interviewed by the newspaper gave her a chance to tell the family story publicly for the press. She is still very proud of the resulting published article.

She keeps a copy of the article framed on her bureau, and photocopies for anyone who expresses interest in the piece. She revels in the minor celebrity status granted to her as an expert on women's rights. She credits the women's movement, as well as the support of her husband, for giving her the courage to open her own business, which she ran for forty years. Also, the newspaper article legitimizes her status as a former business owner as well as a women's rights supporter.

The common element between Eileen's story and Clark's is that the importance of the teller's role in the story is downplayed, which allows others to infer the importance. As with Clark's tale, Eileen's story was told first by several others before she told it herself. Since she was interviewed before and after the publication of the article, its short-term and long-term effects on Eileen's persona could be observed. The telling by others inflates her heroic role. She is described as symbolic of the struggle for women's rights, first spurning the cause, then benefiting from it, and finally championing the movement for others.

More important, staff members, too, are responsive to the effects of the story. Long after its publication, when Eileen experienced another stroke, she was hospitalized for a period of about six weeks when she was able to reap the benefits symbolized by the article. It is the policy of the facility to reassign the room if it will be vacant for more than a few days. Thus, staff members do not encourage residents to become too attached to any one room, reserving the right to move residents at their discretion. However, through special arrangements, Eileen's room was not reassigned when she went into the hospital. When asked why the policy had been ignored in Eileen's case, an administrator gestured toward a copy of the article pinned to the bulletin board in her office and said, "She's important enough to deserve a little extra consideration." With a gesture, she indicates the significance of Eileen's newspaper article as a factor enhancing her status and granting her additional privileges.

Another success story that is legitimized by media attention is the story of Dan and Gerry's wedding. Told by others as an example that it is possible to find happiness in the nursing home, the couple preface the telling of their own tale by showing a videotape of the wedding. With two versions of the tape available, the one they prefer is the shorter version of the ceremony aired by the local television station rather than the one recorded by family members that shows the entire event.

Others talk about Dan and Gerry's wedding more than the couple do themselves. It is not essential to the story that they are lovers in the nursing home, because there are others, nor is it that they are married, because some other residents are also married. What is important is that they met, courted, and married, all within the facility. Furthermore, the event deserved media attention, and it is legitimized by news coverage, which makes it a success story.

Of course, not all of the residents experience celebrity status or legitimation by media attention. Most of them live through their daily routines without ever having known a famous person or having done anything remarkable. However, participating in success stories can also mean telling someone else's story. Relating a success tale, whether derived from media sources or from personal tales about other residents enhances the status of the subject of the narrative by elevating the subject to a heroic level. It also has the additional effect of commenting on the teller. As a parable about life or a comment on one's current situation, success tales strategically enhance the status of the teller by drawing a connection between teller and tale, and drawing attention to the subject of the tale as well.

Chapter 12

Conclusions and Recommendations

A study of media use in the nursing home draws from sources in gerontology, anthropology, communication, and psychology. A summary of the findings provides a starting place for theoretical integration in this final section. Chapter 1 discusses the emergence of a fourth generation which has stimulated growth in the number of facilities that house and accommodate the medical needs of the very old and the physically dependent. However, less attention has been paid to the social needs of nursing home residents than to their medical and custodial care. Largely disconnected from familiar surroundings and support networks, and plagued by physical ailments and psychological vulnerabilities, reestablishing social networks is critical to adjustment to the nursing home. But the tasks associated with this are difficult, if not impossible, for most residents to accomplish.

Chapter 2 develops a literature context for research on media and aging, arguing that media in general and television in particular have a special appeal to the elderly due to their availability and ease of use. Furthermore, the pervasiveness of television has prompted research into the potential for deleterious effects, particularly on the self-concept of a demographic group only marginally recognized by the media industries as an audience. Evaluating the relative importance of all communicative activities, theories of media use tend to portray high media use as solitary, unidimensional, and problematic—a symptom of an unhealthy style of interaction. But more recent research into the social dimensions of media use suggests that media use should be examined as a multidimensional phenomenon that is more complex than single-function theories have suggested. Some individual uses of the media include diversion, enhancing personal identity, and surveillance of the environment. Additionally, social uses include gathering information as a precommunicative act, facilitating communication with others, and promoting social learning.

Media consumption as social action establishes a framework for the examination of mediated communication, advancing the conceptual idea derived from linguistics that premises of action serve as organizing principles to guide individual performance. Premises of action are apparent in the performance of recognizable routines and everyday media practices, and communal themes of action are evident in instances of coordinated and co-oriented action. Therefore, observable acts, the typification scheme used to describe those acts, and the logic used to connect them provide primary focus for the study of media consumption in the nursing home.

Chapter 3 argues for an anthropological methodology organizing the project into three stages of field study, each with its own individual goals, activities, and data. Stage One focuses on background research, gaining entry and acceptance in the facility, beginning observations, and recording fieldnotes. It concludes with a composite day composed of observed media consumption routines, which is representative of the data collected in the first stage. In Stage Two, the research task is to refine interview questions and conduct interviews with nursing home residents. The interviews yield regularities regarding medium and genre preference categories, and they indicate the need for further examination of the relationships in which everyday routines operate. At this stage, relations with roommates are important in determining the amount of consumption as well as the pleasure derived from the media consumption experience. Preliminary conclusions about consumption styles and roommate relations indicate three primary styles—a co-oriented style, a parallel style, and a noncoordinated style of interaction.

In Stage Three of the research project, in-depth interview techniques are adopted with the goal of eliciting accounts of subjective experience from a group of long-term residents. Accounts from eight residents are employed to reveal premises of action that guide the performances of everyday media routines. Premises derived from the interview accounts suggest that media consumption is guided by a variety of strategic goals that include appearing active, maintaining control, and remaining socially integrated. Strategies also include defining intimate space and creating opportunities to interact with others.

Premises of action also reveal some of the values that influence behavior. Stressing the importance of staying busy over idle time, the nursing home residents are sensitive to the cultural ideal that considers high media consumption a poor use of time. They seek to justify that time either through downplaying the importance of it, or even denying that it occurs.

Faced with a number of structural constraints that include failing health, troubled finances, and losses in relationships, nursing home residents strategically counter what they perceive to be negative in their living environment. They actively strive toward maximizing temporal, spatial, and relational resources, and minimizing the constraints with television. Strategies that are used allow consistency with patterns and preferences learned earlier in life. They also allow discussions of tastes to transcend cohort differences in identifying age-specific program trends.

In addition, the notions of withdrawal and disengagement, long criticized in research on aging, can be laid to rest with the adoption of a consistency perspective that shows how obstacles are strategically overcome. The consumption framework is useful for examining consistency because it allows the examination of strategies and practices. Through techniques of observation and interview, accounts reveal the strategic dimensions of communicative behavior.

If audience activity is seen as a social construction, constructs such as media selectivity must be seen to contain social dimensions as well. Also, the term "consumption" implies a physical dimension with both temporal and spatial boundaries. There is a moment both before and after consumption, and a sense for the audience, that some concrete event has transpired in the "here and now." It is from within this broader characterization of the media interaction as consumption that we can better describe the "effect" of the interaction. Media consumption, however, manifests changes in the consumer and the media product, which allows discussion of audience effects without assuming an equivalence with either the producer's intent, or indiscriminately across members of an audience. Effect proceeds through a process wherein the consumer actively engages, retains, creates, and recreates parts of the experience in the memory and behavioral repertoire. However, the site of this production and reproduction is inextricably social. This view of consumption paints the consumer as a rational individual capable of making conscious choices about mediated content, quantity of consumption, and the social circumstances of consumption. However, it is shown in the nursing home environment that this range of choices is severely restricted, that residents are structurally bound by the realities of embodiment, and that the routines of the institution that constrain certain options also empower others. It is through the examination of the stances that nursing home residents assume in relation to the medium and to each other that we can identify sources of individual control in the nursing home.

The idea that social routines both "empower and disable texts" is an important basis of Anderson and Meyer's Accommodation Theory (1988), which sees social routines as primary. Articulating the practices that comprise media consumption is an important task for media research. Also, identifying ways in which consumption is enacted and accomplished by individuals in relation with others leads us away from unidirectional models of media influence toward more useful social constructions.

Anderson and Lorch argue that "viewing" should be conceptualized as a transaction between medium, audience, and context. Likewise, a theoretical view of consumption must consider aspects of the individual, the social and temporal contexts of audience, and the nature of the medium. Therefore, at its most fundamental level a theory of media consumption would have to recognize a degree of agency of audience members, without assuming that the individual is independent from social relations. This recognition takes as a corollary that people have different abilities, reasons, and circumstances for taking part in media-related practices, and these differences will contribute to subjective meaning construction. Also, the intersubjective meaning of media material will be influenced or determined by the social situation and interaction among members of audiences. Furthermore, social situations will in turn influence the perceptual frameworks through which future meaning progresses. The implications of this formulation are in the recognition that audience activity can be heuristically divided into subcomponents for examination. However, in practice, they are linked in the embodiment of individuals and the embeddedness of individuals in the social matrix.

Consumption patterns are socially learned as part of a family, referent group, cohort, and society. Members share mediated experiences, not only of content but as acts of consumption as well. This becomes a part of their identities as individuals and as members within social groupings. Thus, the consumption experience is composed of acts which have meaning that transcends the level of meaning apprehended from the text.

Therefore, the process of media consumption can be examined as it unfolds and is enacted in the contexts of media use. Consumption is both habituated and embodied. Regular enactment of consumption patterns can be empirically observed and documented, enlightening our understanding of mediated communication. As embodied, media consumption practices are lived experience, physically in the here and now and involving coordination and co-orientation. They lead to habituated routines that constitute acts of a certain type. Habituated routines are manifest in patterned interaction and the enactment and observance of rules that are seen to structure the interaction.

Because consumption patterns are socially learned, acquisition is accessible through the examination of instances of instrumental use such as Peterson's analysis of the child's experience of television monsters (1988) and Alexander, Ryan, and Munoz's (1984) analysis of sibling interaction in the media context. Both studies point to the learning of consumption practices and routines and suggest that consumption exhibits a strategic nature. Routines can also intersect with other practices; for example, Hajjar's (1985) study of game playing in the day care television context shows that game playing, gender enactment, and television viewing interact in a system of patterned consumption routines and rituals. These studies illustrate the potential for examining the phenomena of audience constructions and social relations.

Recommendations for future research must point to the need for further exploration of the consumption framework through systematic investigation of the concepts in other settings. Also, knowledge about media consumption strategies can be used to construct a programmatic plan for developing opportunities for social interaction, enhancing self-esteem, and encouraging information pursuit.

Continuing research in the consumption framework established here may also prove beneficial for the advancement of theory in the study of mediated communication. Premises of action yield a consumption logic that is more predictive of media effects than any audience construct currently employed in media research. The stance, used here to build a vocabulary of coordination among audience members, should be subject to further refinement through additional observation and testing. Further research may lead to the identification of additional consumption stances that may ultimately be useful for describing consumption practices among other coordinating audience groups.

In addition, the formulation presented here that strategic use of media can counter what residents perceive as negative about the institutional environment should be pursued in other institutional settings. This perspective can illuminate media routines and social practices in facilities for the care of the elderly as well as in other human service organizations.

Finally, perhaps the most important implications that arise from this study are those that suggest recommendations for changes in the care and treatment of nursing home residents. Three areas in particular should be considered. First, in the area of facility design, nursing homes should be constructed with greater regard to the communicative needs of the aged population who share some common physical barriers. Some of the problems that the media environment can be designed to accommodate are vision and hearing losses, arthritic hands, and limited mobility. Wide-screen televisions, headphone outlets accessible at bedside, oversized remote control devices, and music and videotape libraries are some of the technologies that should be considered in the construction and renovation of nursing homes.

Recommendations in the area of media production must address the lack of programming available to meet the needs of the very old. Knowledge of this audience's consumption styles can inform producers of specialized materials who would consider developing programs with the communication patterns, information processing needs, scheduling difficulties, and tastes and preferences of this audience in mind.

Programming that would facilitate conversation, stimulate mental activity, and suit the aesthetic and intellectual needs of this group would be a welcome addition to the activity repertoire of the nursing home and the members of the elderly population who live more independently in private homes as well.

Final recommendations are in the area of activity planning in the treatment and care of nursing home residents. Where media consumption has often been portrayed as an activity of last resort, a time filler, or a poor use of resources, recognition should be given to the beneficial dimensions of media consumption, and particularly the pleasure derived from its use. Media use textures the communication environment, stimulates conversation, and delivers information and entertainment options. These are important considerations suggesting that media consumption should be valued more positively for its contributions to the quality of nursing home life. Greater recognition for the benefits of media consumption should lead to the adoption of new media-centered activities and especially to the adoption of other therapeutic uses for media materials.

Encouraging the institutionalized elderly to continue previous media consumption practices lessens the feeling that disengagement is expected of them. Furthermore, encouraging the expression of individual tastes and preferences combats some of the negative effects of institutionalization by encouraging external continuity. Individual Commmunication Resource Inventories can suggest areas where the use of media can promote continuity with former lifestyle and encourage the expression of personal tastes. For example, one who used to enjoy the game of golf may no longer be able to play the game, but continuity can be encouraged through a subscription to a golf magazine, by following televised golf tournaments, and even through the use of prerecorded golf videotapes, to the extent that current resources allow.

Caretakers can encourage shared interests and promote the sense of a common bond as well, particularly to encourage bonding between roommate pairs. Shared experiences, among them shared media routines, can result in the establishment of supportive relationships—relationships that can be enabled through the use of television.

Bibliography

Alexander, A., Ryan, M. S., and Munoz, P. (1984). Creating a learning context: Investigations on the interaction of siblings during television viewing. *Critical Studies of Mass Communication, 1*, 345-364.

Allor, M. (1988). Relocating the site of the audience. *Critical Studies of Mass Communication Research, 5*, 217-233.

Altergott, K. (1988). *Daily life in later life.* Newbury Park, CA: Sage.

Anderson, D. R. and Bryant, J. (1983). Research on children's television viewing: The state of the art. In J. Bryant and D. R. Anderson (Eds.) *Children's understanding of television: Research on attention and comprehension.* New York: Academic Press, 331-354.

Anderson, D. R. and Lorch, E. P. (1983). Looking at television: Action or reaction. In J. Bryant and D. R. Anderson (Eds.) *Children's understanding of television: Research on attention and comprehension.* New York: Academic Press, 1-34.

Anderson, J. A. and Meyer, T. P. (1988). *Mediated communication: A social action perspective.* Newbury Park, CA: Sage.

Arling, G. (1976). The elderly widow and her family neighbors and friends. *Journal of Marriage and the Family, 38*, 757-768.

Atchley, R. C. (1974). The meaning of retirement. *Journal of Communication, 24*, 97-100.

Atchley, R. C. (1977). *The social forces in later life: An introduction to social gerontology,* second edition. Belmont, CA: Wadsworth Publishing.

Atchley, R. (1989). A continuity theory of normal aging. *The Gerontologist, 29*, 183-190.

Atkin, C. (1976). Mass media in the aging. In H. J. Oyer and E. J. Oyer (Eds.) *Aging and communication.* Baltimore, MD: University Park Press, 99-118.

Bettinghaus, C. O. and Bettinghaus, E. P. (1976). Communication considerations in the health care of the aging. In H. J. Oyer and E. J. Oyer (Eds.) *Aging and communication.* Baltimore, MD: University Park Press, 129-153.

Beyer, G. and Woods, M. (1963). *Living and activity patterns of the aged.* Research report 6, Center for Housing and Environmental Studies. Ithaca, NY: Cornell University Press.

Biedenharn, P. J. and Normoyle, J. B. (1991). Elderly community residents' reactions to the nursing home: An analysis of nursing home-related beliefs. *The Gerontologist, 31*, 107-114.

Biocca, F. A. (1988). Opposing conceptions of the audience: The active and passive hemispheres of mass communication theory. *Communication Yearbook, 11*, 51-80.

Bitzan, J. E. and Kruzich, J. M. (1990). Interpersonal relationships of nursing home residents. *The Gerontologist, 30*, 385-390.

Blau, Z. (1961). Structural constraints on friendship in old age. *American Sociological Review, 26*, 429-439.

Bliese, N. (1982). Media in the rocking chair: Media uses and functions among the elderly. In G. Gumpert and R. Cathcart (Eds.) *Intermedia: Interpersonal Communication in a Media World*. New York: Oxford University Press, 624-634.

Bogdan, R. and Taylor, S. J. (1975). *Introduction to qualitative research methods: A phenomenological approach to the social sciences*. New York: John Wiley and Sons.

Burgess, R. G. (1984). *In the field: An introduction to field research*. London: George Allen and Unwin.

Chaffee, S. and Wilson, D. (1975). Adult life cycle changes in mass media usage. Paper presented at the annual meeting of the Association for Education in Journalism, Ottawa, Ontario, Canada.

Chown, S. (1981). Friendship in old age. In S. Duck and R. Gilmour (Eds.) *Personal relationships 2: Developing personal relationships*. London: Academic Press, 231-246.

Cowgill, D. and Baulch, N. (1962). The uses of leisure time by older people. *The Gerontologist, 2*, 47-50.

Creecey, R. F. and Wright, R. (1979). Morale and informal activity with friends among black and white elderly. *The Gerontologist, 19*, 544-547.

Cummings, E. and Henry, W. (1961). *Growing old: The process of disengagement*. New York: Basic Books.

Danowski, J. (1975). Informational aging: Interpersonal and mass communication patterns in a retirement community. Paper presented at the annual meeting of the Gerontological Society, Louisville, KY.

De Certeau, M. (1984). *The practice of everyday life*. Translation by S. F. Randall. Berkeley, CA: University of California Press.

De Grazia, S. (1961). The uses of time. In R. W. Kleemeier (Ed.) *Aging and leisure*. New York: Oxford University Press, 113-153.

Douglas, M. and Isherwood, B. (1979). *The world of goods: Towards an anthropology of consumption*. New York: W. W. Norton and Company.

Eco, U. (1980). Toward a semiotic inquiry into the television message. In J. Corner and J. Hawthorn (Eds.) *Communication Studies: A Reader*. London: Edward Arnold.

Erikson, E. H. (1969). Generativity and ego integrity. In B. Neugarten (Ed.) *Middle age and aging*. Chicago: University of Chicago Press, 85-87.

Estes, C. L. (1979). *The aging enterprise*. San Francisco, CA: Jossey-Bass Publishers.

Estes, C. L. and Lee, P. R. (1985). Social, political and economic background of longterm care. In C. Harrington, R. L. Newcomer, C. L. Estes, and Associates (Eds.) *Longterm care of the elderly: Public policy issues*. New York: Sage, 17-40.

Foner, N. (1984). Age and social change. In D. L. Kertzer and J. Keith (Eds.) *Age and anthropological theory.* Ithaca, NY: Cornell University Press, 195-216.

Francher, J. S. (1973). "It's the Pepsi Generation. . . . ": Accelerated aging and the television commercial. *International Journal of Aging and Human Development, 4,* 245-255.

Gerbner, G., Gross, L., Morgan, M., and Signorelli, N. (1994). Growing up with television: The cultivation perspective. In J. Bryant and D. Zillman (Eds.) *Media effects: Advances in theory and research.* Mahwah, NJ: Lawrence Erlbaum.

Gerbner, G., Gross, L., Signorelli, N., and Morgan, M. (1980). Aging with television: Images in television drama and concepts of social reality. *Journal of Communication, 30,* 37-41.

Gerbner, G. and Gross, L. (1976). Living with television: The violence profile. *Journal of Communication, 26,* 173-199.

Graney, M. J. (1975). Media use as a substitute activity in old age. *Journal of Gerontology, 15,* 322-324.

Graney, M. J. and Graney, E. E. (1974). Communication activity substitutions in aging. *Journal of Communication, 24,* 88-96.

Hajjar, W. J. (1985). The engendering process in children viewing television. Unpublished masters thesis, University of Maine, Orono, ME.

Harrington, C., Newcomer, R. L., Estes, C. L., and Associates (1985). *Long-term care of the elderly: Public policy issues.* New York: Sage.

Havighurst, R. J. and Albrecht, R. (1953). *Older people.* New York: Longmans, Green.

Howsden, J. L. (1981). *Work and the helpless self: The social organization of a nursing home.* Chicago, IL: University Press of America.

Ingram, D. K. and Barry, J. R. (1977). National statistics on death in nursing homes: Interpretations and implications. *The Gerontologist, 17,* 303-308.

Kane, R. and Kane, R. A. (1982). *Values and long-term care.* Lexington, MA: Lexington Books.

Kastenbaum, R. and Candy, S. E. (1973). The 4% fallacy: A methodological and empirical critique of extended care facility population statistics. *International Journal of Aging and Human Development, 4,* 15-21.

Kayser-Jones, J. S. (1981). *Old, alone, and neglected: Care of the aged in Scotland and the United States.* Berkley, CA: University of California Press.

Keith, J. (1982). *Old people as people: Social cultural influences on aging and old age.* Boston, MA: Little, Brown.

Keith, J. (1986). Participant observation. In C. L. Fry and J. Keith (Eds.) *New methods for old age research: Strategies for studying diversity.* South Hadley, MA: Bergin and Garvey.

Keith, P. M., Hill, K., Goudy, W. J., and Powers, E. A. (1984). Confidants and well-being: A note on male friendship in old age. *The Gerontologist, 24,* 318-320.

Kemper, P. and Murtaugh, C. M. (1991). Lifetime use of nursing home care. *New England Journal of Medicine, 324*, 595-600.

Korzenny, F. and Nuendorf, K. (1980). Television viewing and self concept of the elderly. *Journal of Communication, 30*, 71-80.

Kubey, R. (1980). Television and aging: Past, present and future. *The Gerontologist, 20*, 16-35.

Lemish, D. (1982). The rules of viewing television in public places. *Journal of Broadcasting, 26*, 757-781.

Lindlof, T. R. (1986). Social and structural constraints of media use in incarceration. *Journal of Broadcasting and Electronic Media, 30*, 341-355.

Lindlof, T. R. (1988). Media audiences as interpretive communities. *Communication Yearbook, 11*, 81-107.

Lofland, J. (1976). *Doing social life: The qualitative study of human interaction in natural settings*. New York: John Wiley and Sons.

Lofland, J. and Lofland, L. H. (1984). *Analyzing social settings: A guide to qualitative observation and analysis*, second edition. Belmont, CA: Wadsworth.

Lo Gerfo, M. (1980). Three ways of reminiscence in theory and practice. *International Journal of Aging and Human Development, 12*, 39-48.

Lull, J. (1980). The social uses of television. *Human Communication Research, 6*, 197-209.

Lull, J. (1982). How families select television programs: A mass-observational study. *Journal of Broadcasting, 26*, 801-811.

McQuail, D. (1985). With benefit of hindsight: Reflections on uses and gratification research. In M. Gurevitch and M. R. Levy (Eds.) *Mass Communication Yearbook, 5*. Newbury Park, CA: Sage, pp. 125-141.

McQuail, D. (1987). *Mass communication theory: An introduction*, second edition. London: Sage.

McQuail, D., Blumer, J. G., and Brown, J. R. (1972). The television audience: A revised perspective. In D. McQuail (Ed.) *Sociology of Mass Communication*. London: Penguin Books, 135-165.

Meyersohn, R. (1961). A critical examination of commercial entertainment. In R. W. Kleemeier (Ed.) *Aging and leisure*. New York: Oxford University Press.

Mitchell, J. and Acuff, G. (1982). Family versus friends: Their relative importance as referent others to an aged population. *Sociological Spectrum, 2*, 367-385.

Morley, D. (1983). Cultural transformations: The politics of resistance. In H. Davis and P. Walton (Eds.) *Language, image, media*. New York: St. Martin's Press.

Morley, D. (1986). *Family television: Cultural power and domestic leisure*. London: Routledge.

Moss, F. E. and Halamandaris, V. J. (1977). *Too old, too sick, too bad: Nursing homes in America*. Germantown, MD: Aspen Systems Corp.

Moss, M. S. and Pfohl, D. C. (1988). New friendships: Staff as visitors of nursing home residents. *The Gerontologist, 28*, 263-265.

Mundorf, N. and Brownell, W. (1990). Media preferences of older and younger adults. *The Gerontologist, 30*, 685-691.

Nussbaum, J. F. (1983). Relational closeness of elderly interaction: Implications for life satisfaction. *The Western Journal of Speech, 47*, 229-243.

Nussbaum, J. F., Thompson, T., and Robinson, J. D. (1989). *Communication and aging*. New York: Harper and Row.

Oyer, H. J. and Oyer, E. J. (1976). *Aging and communication*. Baltimore: University Park Press.

Peck, R. C. (1969). Psychological developments in the second half of life. In B. Neugarten (Ed.) *Middle age and aging*. Chicago: University of Chicago Press, 88-92.

Peterson, E. (1987). Media consumption and girls who want to have fun. *Critical Studies of Mass Communication, 4*, 37-50.

Peterson, E. (1988). The technology of media consumption. *American Behavioral Scientist, 32*, 156-168.

Peterson, M. (1973). The visibility and image of old people on television. *Journalism Quarterly, 50*, 568-573.

Peterson, R. A. (1982). Measuring culture, leisure and time use. In D. C. Whitney and E. Wartella (Eds.) *Mass Communication Yearbook, 3*. Beverly Hills: Sage, 445-462.

Radway, J. (1984). *Reading the romance*. Chapel Hill, NC: University of North Carolina Press.

Radway, J. (1987). Where is the field?: Ethnography, audiences and the redesign of research practice. Paper presented at the annual meeting of the International Communication Association, Montreal, Canada, May, 1987.

Real, M. R., Anderson, H., and Harrington, M. H. (1980). Television access for older adults. *Journal of Communication, 30*, 81-88.

Rice, D. P. (1985). Healthcare needs of the elderly. In C. Harrington, R. L. Newcomer, C. L. Estes, and Associates (Eds.) *Long-term care of the elderly: Public policy issues*. New York: Sage, 41-66.

Roberto, K. A. and Scott, J. P. (1984-1985). Friendship patterns among older women. *International Journal of Aging and Human Development, 19*, 1-10.

Rowles, G. D. (1978). *Prisoners of space: Exploring the geographical experience of older people*. Boulder, CO: Western Press.

Rubin, A. M., Perse, E. M., and Powell, R. A. (1985). Loneliness, parasocial interaction, and local television news viewing. *Human Communication Research, 12*, 155-180.

Schramm, W. (1969). Aging and mass communication. In M. W. Riley, J. W. Riley, and M. E. Johnson (Eds.) *Aging and Society, Volume 2*. New York: Russell Sage Foundation, 353-375.

Schreiber, E. and Boyd, D. (1980). How the elderly perceive television commercials. *Journal of Communication, 30*, 61-70.

Shield, R. R. (1988). *Uneasy endings: Daily life in an American nursing home*. Ithaca, NY: Cornell University Press.

Sigman, S. J. (1982). Some communicational aspects of patient placement and careers in two nursing homes. Unpublished dissertation, Philadelphia, PA: The Graduate School, University of Pennsylvania.

Swan, J. H. and Harrington, C. (1985). Medicaid nursing home reimbursement policies. In C. Harrington, R. L. Newcomer, C. L. Estes, and Associates (Eds.) *Longterm care of the elderly: Public policy issues*. New York: Sage, 125-152.

Tamir, L. M. (1979). *Communication and the aging process: Interaction throughout the life cycle*. New York: Pergamon.

Tesch, S., Whitbourne, S. K., and Nehrke, M. F. (1981). Friendship, social interaction and subjective well-being of older men in an institutional setting. *International Journal of Aging and Human Development, 13*, 317-327.

Tobin, S. S. (1980). Institutionalization of the aged. In N. Datan and N. Lohmann (Eds.) *Transitions of aging*. New York: Academic Press, 195-211.

Unruh, D. R. (1983). *Invisible lives: Social worlds of the aged*. Beverly Hills, CA: Sage.

Van Maanen, J. (1983). The fact of fiction in organizational ethnography. In Van Maanen, J. (Ed.) *Qualitative methodology*, Beverly Hills, CA: Sage, 37-55.

Vladeck, B. C. (1980). *Unloving care: The nursing home tragedy*. New York: Basic Books.

Wenner, L. (1976). Functional analysis of TV viewing for older adults. *Journal of Broadcasting, 20*, 77-88.

Wingard, D. L., Jones, D. W., and Kaplan, R. M. (1987). Institutional care utilization by the elderly: A critical review. *The Gerontologist, 27*, 156-163.

Index

Page numbers followed by the letter "i" indicate illustrations; those followed by the letter "t" indicate tables.

Accommodation Theory, 138
Activity calendar
  importance of, 27
  use of, 114-115
Activity room, use of, 35,43-44,104
Activity theory, 9
Adelle
  Hilltop routine, 37,44
  key informant, 78-80
Adjustment, nursing home, 57
Affiliation/avoidance, relational use, 17
Aging
  communication decline in, 11
  continuity theory of, 19-20,23-24
  nursing homes, 3
Alice, roommate style, 59-60,60i
American Movie Classics (AMC), viewing of, 33,50,54
Anthropological method, nursing home research, 21-22
Anticipated media use, 90
"Around the World," 27-28
Arts & Entertainment (A&E) channel, 50
Attentive stance, 94,96

Ball games, viewing of, 35,36-37, 111,112. *See also* Sports, viewing of
Barbara
  Hilltop routine, 35,43-44
  media usage of, 93-95,97
Barnaby Jones, 50

Bea
  Hilltop routine, 35,43
  media usage of, 93,94,97
Bert
  Hilltop routine, 32-33,35,43,44
  key informant, 75-78
  local information, 51
  roommate style, 60-61
  television viewing, 110
Bible study, 68,115
Big, 120
Bingo game, 36,38,68,115

Cable News Network (CNN), viewing of, 33,34,50
Cartoons, viewing of, 37
CBS, preference for, 50
Charlie, Hilltop routine, 35-37,44
Cigarettes, 32,42,43
Clark
  daily activity, 108
  Hilltop routine, 35-37,44
  key informant, 66,80-82
  media stories, 130-132,133
  roommate style, 58-59,59i,61,63
  routine, 107
Cognitive processing, issue of, 95,96
Collins, Floyd, 128-129
Communication
  activities, evaluation of, 8-9
  facilitation, relational use, 17
  and gerontology, 2-3,5
  practices, 2

149

Competence/dominance, relational use, 17
Consumption periodicity, 106,110
Consumption strategies, 87,90, 136-137,139. *See also* Stances, media usage
Continuity theory, 19-20
Control
 exercise of, 101,137
 obstacles to exercising, 117
Coordinated consumption, 98,99,136
Coordination, 87,93,94,139
Co-orientation, 58,59i,61,136,139
Craft activity, 69,71,92
Crime, increased fear of, 8
Current Affair, viewing of, 40
Current Events, 39,40,41

Dan
 domesticity, 117-118
 establishing a routine, 105-106
 Hilltop routine, 33,41-43,44
 key informant, 82-84
 media stories, 133-134
 obstacles, 117
 schedule, 115-116
Day care, elderly in, 1
Dementia, television use and, 8,76
Depression, television use and, 8
"Disciplined abstractions," 48
Diversion, gratification component, 17,135
Domestic routines, coordination of, 57,62,86

Eileen
 Hilltop routine, 39-41,44
 key informant, 69-72
 media stories, 132-133
 reading, 52
 roommate style, 59-60,60i
Elderly
 media consumption of, 2,7-12,135

Elderly *(continued)*
 in nursing homes, 13-14
 television preferences, 8,12
 television use by, 7-12,14,135
Embodied consumption, 139
Entertainment Tonight, 116
Enunciation, 98
Environmental resource, media as, 17
Estelle
 activities, 114-115
 control, 101-102
 Hilltop routine, 38-39,44,66-69
 key informant, 66-69
 listening to music, 54
 local information, 51
 media stories, 127-128
Euchre, male socializing, 35

Field trips
 desire for, 106-107
 special events, 114
Fourth generation, emergence of, 1,135
Frail elderly
 care of, 1
 nursing home residents, 13
"Free time," 107
Friendship, in nursing homes, 15-16

Game shows, viewing of, 35,39,52, 94. *See also* Quiz shows
Gender, television choices and, 111,112
Gerontology, and communications, 2-3,5
Gerry
 Hilltop routine, 41-43,44
 key informant, 66,82-84
 media stories, 133-134
 reading, 52
Gilyard, Darrell, 127
Gone with the Wind, 119
Guest speakers, special event, 114
Guiding Light, The, 91

Index

Habituated consumption, 139
Harlequin romance novels, reading of, 34-35,74,91
Helen, media usage of, 97
Highway to Heaven, 50,116,126
Hilltop
    afternoon television, 37,39,44
    breakfast television, 34,43
    description of, 24,26
    early television, 32-34,43
    evening television, 40,41,55,58, 60,61-62
    lunch, 35-36
    media availability at, 26
    morning television, 35
    routine activity at, 26-27
Hit Parade, 54
Hitchhiking stance, 95,98
How-to-shows, elderly interest in, 8

Identity, 23-24,125-126,129-130
Independence, social status and, 26
Individual Communication Resource Inventory, 24,25t,141
Institutionalization
    nursing homes, 3
    predictors of, 14
Interventions, 2
Interview protocol, 47-48

Jeopardy, 50
Jerry, roommate style, 58-59,59i,61

Key informants
    description of, 65-66
    selection of, 27,29

Ladies Circle, 115
Ladies Home Journal, 49,91
Lawrence Welk Show, 50,53
Lillian, Hilltop routine, 33-34,43

Local information, desire for, 50-51
Lull, James, 16-18

Mae West, 130,131,132
Magazines, reading of, 49,73-74
Margaret
    Hilltop routine, 33-35,43
    key informant, 72-75
    media stories, 128-129
    television viewing, 112-113
Matlock, viewing of, 41
McClure, Jessica, 128,129
Mealtime, role of, 36,44
Media
    Adelle's use of, 79-80
    Bert's use of, 78,79,109-110
    Charlie's use of, 95,111-112
    Clark's use of, 81-82,109,111-112
    Dan's use of, 82-83,104,122
    Eileen's use of, 72
    Estelle's use of, 68-69,92,95, 114-115
    Gerry's use of, 82-83,104,122
    Margaret's use of, 74-75,91,95
    stories, value of, 126,129
    use, types of, 90
Media consumption
    nursing homes, 3
    recalled, 90,91,92-93
    social dimension of, 16,86
    types of, 98
Messiah (Handel), 53
Microwave oven, use of, 77
Mobility
    impact on friendship, 15-16
    limitations of, 108
Monitoring stance, 94-95,98,113
Movie attendance, elderly decline in, 8
Movies, viewing of, 52,54,117, 118-122
Murder She Wrote, 50
Music, listening to, 53-54
Musical programs, special events, 114

Nashville Network, The (TNN),
    viewing of, 38
Network television, viewing of, 50
Networking, 28
News, viewing of, 33,34,41,52-53,73
Newspaper, reading of, 34,38-39,40,
    51-52,69,71
Noncoordinated orientation, 60-61
Nonselective consumption, 90,101
Nursing home resident, typical, 14
Nursing homes
    common complaints in, 126
    elderly in, 13
    gerontology practice and, 1
    as home, 31
    as medical institution, 31
    projected need for, 13-14
    recommendations for change,
        140-141
    research protocol, 22-23
    resident control within, 102-103
    television use in, 1-2

Old-Time Gospel Hour, 127
Oprah Winfrey Show, 38

Parallel consumption, 98
Parallel orientation, 59-60,60i,136
Peer group interaction, 14-15
Personal expression, opportunities
    for, 125
Personal identity, gratification
    component, 17,135-136
Personal relationships, gratification
    component, 17
Phyllis, media use of, 120,122,123
Price is Right, The, 115
Privacy, 84,103-104
"Privatization," 10
Public media event, definition of, 27
Public Television, viewing of, 50

Quiz shows, elderly interest in, 8.
    See also Game shows

Radio, listening to, 43,53,76,81-82
    elderly decline in, 8
Ralph, Hilltop routine, 35-36
Reader's Digest, 37,49
Reading
    inhibitions to, 52
    time spent in, 49,52,73,81-82,83
Reciprocal friendships, 15
Regulative, media's, 17
Relational use, media's, 17
Relationships, types of at Hilltop, 44
Religious programming, viewing
    of, 39,54,114
Research site, description of, 24,26.
    See also Hilltop
Resources
    availability of, 102-103
    elderly and, 12
"Restorative self-nurturing," 63
Roommates
    satisfaction with, 54-55
    styles of, 58-61
Roosevelt, Franklin D., 132
Routines, establishing, 105,138
Ruth, media use of, 120-122

Secondary activity, television
    viewing as, 92
Selective consumption, 90
Selectivity, 87,116
    impediments to, 118
    option of, 102,137-138
Self-concept, lowered, 7-8,10,12,135
Self-esteem, nursing home residents,
    15
"Self-improvement," 63
Semantic production, 95-96
700 Club, 54
Situation comedies, viewing of, 52
Sleeping patterns, nursing home, 118
Soap operas, viewing of, 35,38,50,
    52,68,91,94,111,112

Social action, 23
Social activity, television and, 22
Social disengagement, 9-10,11,12
Social learning, relational use, 17
Social participation, motivation for, 19
Social withdrawal. *See* Social disengagement
Sound of Music, The, 54
Special events, 114
Sports, viewing of, 77,111,112. *See also* Ball games, viewing of
Stances, media usage, 93-95,97,140
Structural constraints, 9,19
Surveillance, gratification component, 17,136

Taste culture, 18
Taste homophily, 18
Television
 creation of privacy with, 104
 elderly use of, 2,7-12,14,135
 as media substitute, 54
 preferences of elderly, 89-90
 protocol for evaluating, 22
 relationships and, 85
 social use model, 16-17
 time spent in viewing, 49-50,73,76
 typical nursing home resident, 14,135-136

Television *(continued)*
 view of elderly use of, 8,135
Televisions, placement at Hilltop, 26
Tenure, 57,65
Tonight Show, The, 43
"Trajectory," 62
Turner and Hootch, 43
TV Guide, 33,41,49,52,76,106,115

USA Today, reading of, 40

"Vanishing breed," 8
Vicarious mobility, 108
Videotapes, 42-43
"Viewing," 138-139

Weather Channel, The, 50
Weather information, viewing of, 34,73
Welk, Lawrence, acquaintance with, 132
Wheel of Fortune, viewing of, 40,50,115
Witnessing stance, 93,94,98
Women's movement, 132-133

Young-elderly, television use of, 11